1470

the sex doctors

in the basement

villard

NEW YORK

the
sex
doctors

in the
basement

TRUE STORIES
FROM A
SEMI-CELEBRITY
CHILDHOOD

molly jong-fast

Published in the United States by Villard Books,
an imprint of The Random House Publishing Group,
a division of Random House, Inc., New York.

VILLARD and "V" CIRCLED Design are
registered trademarks of Random House, Inc.

Library of Congress Cataloging-in-Publication Data
Jong-Fast, Molly
    The sex doctors in the basement: true stories from a semi-
celebrity childhood / Molly Jong-Fast.—1st ed.
        p. cm.
    ISBN 1-4000-6144-X
        1. Jong-Fast, Molly, 1978—Childhood and youth.
    2. Novelists, American—20th century—Biography. 3. Jong-
    Fast, Molly, 1978—Psychology. 4. Bohemianism—United
    States. I. Title.
    PS3560.O57Z465 2004
    813'.54—dc22   2004043056

Villard Books website address: www.villard.com

Printed in the United States of America on acid-free paper

9 8 7 6 5 4 3 2 1

FIRST EDITION

Book design by Gretchen Achilles

To my father, who supports me,

my husband, who writes me,

and my stepfather, who represents me.

contents

✳

Why I Wrote This Book   *xi*

The Optimistic Lesbian   3

I Caught the Bouquet at
My Grandfather's Wedding   19

Heavenly Hash   35

How to Get Famous Without
Really Trying   49

The Gentle Gentile   66

The Sex Doctors in the Basement   80

How an Obese, Muumuu-Wearing
Fascist Helped Me Lose Weight   96

Mom's Fourth Chance at Happiness   110

My New Daddy Is a Jailbird or
Perhaps an Italian Playboy   122

contents

My Brief Life with a Model   135

What's in Joan Collins's Box?   149

Venice   162

Grandpa   176

Acknowledgments   *191*

why i wrote this book

*

WHEN I SAY TO PEOPLE, "I'm working on a book of essays about my childhood," the statement gives them pause. They smile at me. They've thought all along that I was a no-trick pony dining out on the family secrets. Well, I have news for them: I am a one-trick pony dining out on sushi and Tasti D-Lite.

But my one-trick pony–ness has nothing to do with why I wrote this book. I wrote this book because I had a sordid tale to tell: a tale of sex doctors who lived in our basement and of a potential stepfather who went to jail for hiding wine under the Thames, a tale of a lesbian grandaunt who dallied with a male rabbi and a Communist grandpa whose continued obsession with the Trotskyites caused him much distress.

Sure, I met with adversity when I sat down to write this memoir; for instance, I had to fight the fact that I have no idea what normal is. I think I should just get that out in the open, especially since you are about to read my memoir. I grew up in a town house with a pink door. I thought Doctor Ruth was a kindly old granny and not a boiling cauldron of potent, passionate, and instructive sexuality. Let me just clarify that normal waved bye-bye to me a long time ago (although probably not as long ago as it deserted Grandpa Howie—Howard Fast, author of *Spartacus*—who believed that Walter Cronkite and Nancy Reagan were in fact the same person).

Ultimately I wrote this memoir to set the record crooked. I wrote this book to help the children of the sort-of-famous. I wrote this to deal with my childhood. Perhaps the problem was not that I had a famous mother but that I didn't have a famous enough mother. Perhaps not being in the spotlight enough had ruined me from a young age. Had my mom been Goldie Hawn, think of how much weller I might be now.

I also wrote this memoir to answer the question that everyone has been dying to know the answer to:

"So what's it like being the daughter of the Queen of Erotica?"

This question was asked me by, among others, a British interviewer whom I met at a literary festival in the English countryside. She had nails like Barbra Streisand in *The Prince of Tides*. I thought she was talking about someone else.

"Tell me, do men want to sleep with you because you're Erica Jong's daughter?"

"Sure, all the time. Why just last week some guy was like, hey, your mother wrote an erotic novel in the seventies, let's go do it."

"But really, how does it feel to be a sex queen's daughter?"

"Once in science class when I was in the fifth grade this kid said to me, 'Your mom writes dirty books.' I was really a tattle-tale, so I went to the teacher and said something to her about this boy, and the teacher, who may have been a born-again Christian, said, 'Well, your mother *does* write dirty books.' " That teacher always was mean to me. Maybe it was because once I asked her if she was pregnant and it turned out she wasn't.

Years later, I found myself in a position similar to that teacher's (except I was pregnant). I finally understand what it's like to be a fat ass.

And yet I still really don't understand my bohemian childhood. After reading these sordid tales, maybe *you* will understand why I am mildly maladjusted. If you do manage to make sense of all of this, then perhaps you can call me and together we can try to love again. Or maybe you can buy me a pony. Pleeaaase!

the sex doctors

in the basement

the optimistic lesbian

※

THERE ARE A LOT of brilliant doctors and scientists in the Jong family. The Jong family is also chock-full of great gourmet chefs and talented tennis players. Members of the Jong family are placid and sane; they enjoy large family dinners and even larger family reunions. Almost every single member of the Jong family is Chinese. Tragically, this family full of good-looking, tennis-playing, well-adjusted Chinese doctors is no relation to my actual family. My mother's married name was Jong, and she acquired it during her second marriage, a brief legal coupling with an even briefer Chinese shrink. Sadly, my mother's maiden name was Mann, and her mother's maiden name was Mirsky.

Where the Jongs play tennis, the Mirskys play "ride the porcelain pony" while they suffer the effects of our two biggest inheritances—irritable bowel syndrome and Crohn's disease. While the Jongs are perfecting the latest gourmet dish, the Mirskys are screaming at Lulu (the illegal Ecuadorian housekeeper) and chugging Manischewitz. While the Jongs are diagnosing cancers and radiating tumors, the Mirskys are being diagnosed with everything from West Nile virus to hepatitis C (sorry, Uncle Larry).

It all started with two Polacks. Great-Grandpa Mirsky had two daughters, Eda, my grandmother, and Kitty, my grandaunt. Both girls were born in England, and both came to New York City via Ellis Island before they were ten years old.

In the grand tradition of sisters, Eda and Kitty always hated each other. Mostly they hated each other because they did the same thing; both of them were painters. Grandma Eda painted flowers and children. Grandma's flower paintings were filled with lavish colors, sensuous shapes, and the hand of her abused housekeeper, who'd been holding the flowers since early the day before. Grandma's flower paintings were the stuff of midwestern hotel room walls. But Grandma's portraits of her children and grandchildren seemed to express something more than just a love of flowers or housekeepers: Grandma's paintings of her family highlighted her distaste for motherhood. For example, the only portrait Grandma painted of me showed me with hooved feet, horns, and hair made entirely of writhing snakes.

Kitty painted different subject matter. She painted dark, brooding seascapes. She painted the howling wind, the waves slamming into Fire Island, the spray from a huge hurricane-force wind, the harsh sand, and the pain she felt about the popularity of the song "Abra-abra-cadabra, I want to reach out and grab ya." She also painted the occasional kitten.

Each sister thought the other's work was of the hack-neyed greeting-card sort.

Once I interrupted Grandma's screaming about socialism long enough to ask her why she didn't like Kitty. It was the late eighties. I remember little of that dark time in American history, except that I had feathered hair and thought white Keds worn with scrunchy socks were fashion-forward. Grandma was standing half-clad in a red silk Japanese kimono on a foot ladder in the bathroom of her apartment on ritzy Central Park West, where all the window curtains were made of old floral bedsheets, and all the toilet seats were painted with large red and pink daisies. Grandma had a stomach that looked like a tushy placed slightly higher up on the wrong side of her body. Through all clothing—sweaters, coats, dresses, and heavy wool cardigans—one could see Grandma's enor-mous front tushy. Grandma had gotten rich by Grandpa's foray into tchotchkes (Grandpa had started an import-export business aptly named Seymour Mann Imports), which had happened innocently enough when one night after smoking tea Grandpa had come home stoned with a showgirl on each arm. Grandma didn't like showgirls. She didn't like her hus-band bringing two of them home when she was busy with two other girls, her young daughters. The showgirl incident basically marked the end of Grandpa's career as a drummer.

Yes, Grandpa had been a drummer; he had played in a Cole Porter review. He was immensely proud of his time as a drummer, but his first career was only ever apparent to me in one way—he was almost completely deaf. So deaf when he picked up the phone the first thing he would say was "I'm fine."

Grandma and Grandpa's apartment at 25 Central Park West always smelled of sweet, brown, fibrous stewed prunes. Asked why she did not like Grand-Aunt Kitty, Grandma Eda turned to me violently, thus accidentally (I hope) revealing her ample though sagging bosom, and replied, "She believes everything is good."

Grandma Eda disliked Kitty because Kitty was an optimist. Grandma knew life was broken into three categories—the horrible, the miserable, and the stupid. Naturally people who believed otherwise always fell into the last category. Hence Kitty's belief in the goodness of kittens (especially those painted on black velvet) was proof positive that she was a moron. Grandma blamed Kitty's optimism on her being a lesbian.

Anyway, Kitty came to America, painted, fought with and generally hated her sister, and then married a man named Dayton Brandfield, and . . . "WAIT!" you scream. "How can this be?" you ask yourself and the man sitting next to you on the Number 6 train, who smells of coconut aftershave. Didn't I just tell you that Kitty was an optimist, therefore a lesbian? Well, in the Mirsky family, you can be gay, but that does not excuse you from your constitutional duty to marry and pass on those irritable-bowel-syndrome genes (though Kitty never did have any children). Dayton was a painter, but then he got into the marketing and selling of little objects like battery boxes, otherwise known as tchotchkes. Tchotchkes were not good to Dayton, although it does sound from all the very reliable family testimonials about him that Dayton was no great rocket scientist, no Stephen Hawking, and not even a Noelle Bush, for that matter. And so, after Dayton failed at tchotchkes, *at the ripe old age of forty,* Grand-Aunt Kitty dumped Dayton to love the ladies.

From then on Kitty rode the pink pussy express. The first thing she did was move. Optimistic lesbians aren't allowed to live on the Upper East or Upper West Side, they must live in Chelsea. The next thing Kitty did was find a place on Fire Island; all optimistic lesbians must have summer places on Fire Island. After that she bought a giant papier-mâché lion. This is crucial: 90 percent of all optimistic lesbians have at least one papier-mâché lion in their Chelsea apartments. The last thing Kitty did was find a lesbian lover: all optimistic lesbians have to have lesbian lovers; otherwise, they're just *gay till graduation,* like some students at certain liberal arts colleges (Smith, Wesleyan, Oberlin, Vassar, et cetera).

And so life went on for Kitty Brandfield. She painted dark, brooding, despairing, feeling, crying, dying, sensitive, earth-changing, world-altering seascapes and the occasional happy kitten. She lived on Fire Island in the summers and frolicked with the other optimistic lesbians and with Calvin Klein. She lived in Chelsea in the winter and ate stale stuffed lobster at the Chelsea Hotel, while Sid and Nancy were upstairs killing each other. As in any good feud, Grandma Eda continued to hate Grand-Aunt Kitty, and Grand-Aunt Kitty continued to not quite understand why Grandma hated her. Grand-Aunt Kitty's days were filled with all these things and with munching at the Y.

Mom dragged me to visit Kitty a few times in her loft in Chelsea. I hated visiting Kitty because she smelled bad, fed me weird stewed fruits, and pinched my cheeks. If Grand-Aunt Kitty had been a large-screen TV or had fed me huge quantities of chocolate, I might have loved her. Kitty would let me sit on the giant papier-mâché lion while she and Mom talked. Sadly, Kitty's lion was also not TV.

"Well, Erica . . ." Kitty had a long, wrinkly neck like a turkey (in the spirit of karma I will probably have a neck twice as bad, so long and wrinkly that it touches the floor when I talk). "I . . ." And then Kitty would say something chockablock with ambiguity. Truly, I think one of the reasons Grandma hated Kitty was that Kitty was just totally unable to say anything without some degree of Al Gore–ish mealy-mouthedness. Where Grandma would say, "How did you get so fat?" Kitty would say, "Maybe you might have put on a little weight or maybe not. Maybe my eyesight is going, maybe that's what it is."

One note on the physical composition of members of the Mirsky family: Great-Grandpa Mirsky lived to be 99 years old. His father lived to be 210 years old. His father's father was Moses. Unfortunately, Great-Grandpa Mirsky was not a charming old gentleman like, say, that lovable guntoter Charlton Heston or the cuddly Star Wars monger Ronald Reagan. Great-Grandpa Mirsky was addicted to kicking puppies, kittens, and goldfish.

Possibly the most interesting fact of the whole Great-Grandpa Mirsky debacle is that the puppy-kicking activities of his later years were actually a dramatic improvement over his youth. The same fact was true for Grandma Eda, who magically became a fuzzy and cuddly ninety-year-old with the help of dementia, a few minor falls in Central Park, and Prozac.

Kitty was about eighty when she forgot her name. Then,

a few days later, she forgot everything about herself—where she lived, how old she was, where she kept her trusty bottle of the Jewish Jim Beam (Manischewitz), what her favorite fruit was, whether she preferred Sonny or Cher, and the angst she had felt about little kittens being so incredibly cute. She forgot about her deep and meaningful friendship with Calvin Klein (so did he). Each day washed more facts from her brain, and soon Kitty had invited a very pleasant young homeless man to come and live in her stark, still pretty much unconverted, steam-heated, concrete-floored, industrial Chelsea loft that had once been a circus peanut–candy factory.

Now we porn-writing toilet-seat-decorating Polacks aren't exactly in the Social Register, and I actually have dated a few homeless men from time to time (positives about dating the homeless—no pesky utility bills, plenty of time to lavish attention on you, no place they need to be). But that said, taking a stray homeless person in to live with you can really be ill-advised.

Mom was not happy to hear that Kitty had invited a homeless man to come and live with her. Mom and her two sisters decided something had to be done. Around the time that Kitty lost her memory, her much younger girlfriend left her for Chastity Bono (blatant libelous falsehood). The sisters (Mom, Aunt Nana, and Aunt Claudia) found themselves in a sticky wicket not completely unlike the situation in *King Lear,* except with extra complications, like department stores calling them about special events, therapists selling them hours that were only forty minutes, and the difficulty of getting their children into Manhattan private schools.

Something had to be done! Grand-Aunt Kitty couldn't

just wander the streets looking for good-looking homeless men. That was my job. And so Grand-Aunt Kitty went to the place where all old people go when they're too poor to live in Palm Beach and too homosexual to live in West Palm Beach: a classy nursing home in the Bronx.

Not just any classy nursing home in the Bronx would be good enough for a Mirsky. Our family's strict requirements were that there had to be famous people in the nursing home, and furthermore, it had to have famous people or relatives of famous people living in it, and did I mention the part about the famous people?

Luckily, there are many families as classy as the Mirsky family. And they send their relatives to the Hebrew Home for the Aged in Riverdale. The best and the brightest aging, middle-class, incontinent Jews end up at the Hebrew Home.

But who are these celebrities whose very presence is assurance to us that our elder will get the best care? Barbara Walters's mother lives (breathes, anyway) at the Hebrew Home for the Aged. So do Uri Geller's mom and Henry Kissinger's flamboyant second cousin.

And so Grand-Aunt Kitty moved into the Hebrew Home for the Aged in Riverdale. Various members of the family had various crises of conscience about putting Kitty in a home, but we were all able to reassure ourselves that if it was good enough for Barbara Walters's mom, then it was good enough for Aunt Kitty. Besides Aunt Kitty wasn't even sure who any of us were, so she couldn't actively try to make us feel guilty.

And so Aunt Kitty moved from Chelsea to Riverdale. She moved from an industrial loft to a place where captains of industry wore diapers. She moved from a life that resembled the musical *Rent* to a life that looked more like the musical *Urinetown*. She had to get rid of the large papier-mâché lion, but she didn't lose her optimism or her lesbianism.

Not right away, anyway.

Can I just interrupt for one second with a very telling sidebar, please? I recently visited my ninety-one-year-old grandma Eda and discovered a copy of *Beyond Viagra* on my grandpa's bedside table. Grandpa was at work, so I was unable to question him about this startling (and needless to say very disturbing) revelation. I did ask my mom about *Beyond Viagra*. She smiled in a very *Our Bodies, Ourselves* way and said, "When you're ninety, you'll be happy if you can have sex with or without lubricant, Viagra, or the assistance of a nurse practitioner."

But back to Kitty: Kitty spent her days at the Maurice R. Greenberg Wellness Center, which according to the Hebrew Home's website (www.hebrewhome.org), "offers sophisticated exercise equipment and innovative fitness programs that are tailored to meet the individual's needs." She also enjoyed "the nationally renowned art collection, as well as numerous other displays of art, antiquities, live birds and fish. . . ." Nothing says "Barbara Walters's mother lives here" like live birds and fish. And then there's always "The Dorothy Doughty porcelain bird collection, one of only two complete and undamaged collections in the world." Not exactly kittens, but at least kittens (the ones in cartoons anyway) eat birds.

She seemed to love life there (who knows?), day in day out, in the Bronx, listening to bad classical music, celebrating all the Jewish holidays (most of which, being the most reformed of reformed Jews, she'd never even heard of). She seemed to like the art therapy, the play therapy, the paper-crumbling arthritis therapy, the coping-with-incontinence classes, and the lying around waiting for God to take her to his kingdom. And if she had been a normal octogenarian, that might have been enough. But of course it wasn't enough, because Kitty was a Mirsky and a lesbian, until one day.

One day about a year after she had moved into the Hebrew Home for the Aged in Riverdale, Mom went to visit Kitty. It was a sunny day in June; Mom drove straddling both lanes on the Hutchinson Parkway. Mom parked, taking up three parking spaces, and then went in to visit Grand-Aunt Kitty. She had brought her some paints. She looked around for Barbara Walters.

She knocked on Kitty's door. She found the door to Kitty's room ajar. Being a Mirsky, she pushed the door, and it swung open. And there was Grand-Aunt Kitty orally servicing a . . . rabbi. And not a female rabbi, who might have been an appropriate mate for a lesbian aunt, but a male rabbi. Okay, just for common decency's sake and so that my grandparents don't disinherit me (your li'l Moll–Moll loves you, Grammy), Grand-Aunt Kitty wasn't actually Monica Lewinskying; she was just holding hands with the aforementioned rabbi and leaning her head against his shoulder.

Mom was shocked, and few things shock Mom (she was shocked when her first husband thought he was Jesus and wanted to walk out the twenty-fifth-floor window, and she was also shocked by the quality of Dart's vacuum-packed meats (please see "The Gentle Gentile"), the success of *The Simple Life* with Paris Hilton, and the fall of the Iron Curtain).

"But, Kitty!" Mom said, staring at her lesbian aunt.

"Ohh, look, it's the nice black nurse, she's come to change my diapers," Kitty said to her rabbinically inclined companion, looking at Mom.

But Mom's not black. Not to say there aren't black Jews: Sammy Davis, Jr., is Jewish, and Lenny Kravitz is half Jewish. Bea Arthur is also Jewish, but she's unfortunately not black, though she was on *The Golden Girls,* which was meant to be based in Miami, where Puff Daddy sometimes hangs out.

And Mom's not a nurse. This is not to say that writers can't be nurses (Philip Roth once had sex with a nurse, and Norman Mailer stabbed his second or third wife).

And Grand-Aunt Kitty was supposed to be gay. Not to say that there aren't gay women who decide they are straight (Anne Heche decided she was straight after not sleeping for days and drinking a ton of coffee and wandering the streets talking about how she was from Mars, a claim many believed).

Mom left that day slightly disturbed about the whole debacle. She immediately brought it up with her two sisters. It was important for the Mirsky family to ask itself, how did this happen? The sisters had a telephone powwow. The most important fact about my mother and her two sisters is that they look like triplets. All three of them are attractive women of medium height with wavy blond hair and blue eyes. All three of them have lived similar lives, except that one of them (my mother) has written books that have sold over 30 million copies, and another (Aunt Nana) married an agriculturalist from Beirut and lived through the Lebanese civil war, with snipers picking her neighbors off on their way to the supermarket. But whatever their differences in temperament and experience, all three sisters agreed about Aunt Kitty. The general consensus was that Grand-Aunt Kitty's sexuality had gone the way of our names, our faces, and where she hid the Manischewitz. Alzheimer's disease had made Grand-Aunt Kitty forget that she was gay. And Alzheimer's had also convinced Kitty that Mom was a black nurse.

Aunt Kitty continued to live at the Hebrew Home for the Aged in Riverdale. She continued to paint and to try to get in good with Barbara Walters's mother. She continued to do everything the same way, except Kitty stopped munching carpet and started having gentlemen callers. Apparently the Hebrew Home for the Aged is an excellent place for sleeping around, like a big ongoing frat party.

This continued until Aunt Kitty died.

It was a shock: one day she was an eighty-five-year-old, incontinent Alzheimer's sufferer living in a nursing home, and the next she was dead. It really makes you think. It makes you want to live life to the fullest. We were all shocked. I personally was shocked 'cause I thought she'd been dead for years.

We planned the funeral. There are only a few chic places to be embalmed in Manhattan. For the goyim, Franky Campbell's is a nice place to have your blood drained and replaced with formaldehyde. Franky's is all about location; it's right on Madison Avenue, nestled between Agnès B. and Betsey Johnson, close to E.A.T. food and across the street from the Paul Stuart women's store. This location makes it possible to both shop and mourn. Some Jews like to memorialize at Franky Campbell's, but it's kind of like changing your name from Ralph Lipshitz to Ralph Lauren and trying to get into the "take no Jews" Maidstone Club. The really chic place to be memorialized if you're a Jew is Temple Emmanuel, a limestone temple on Fifth Avenue that Ron Perlman frequents. Unfortunately, my family (as I mentioned earlier) was a family of toilet-painting Polack pornographers, so we ended up celebrating the life of Kitty Brandfield at Riverside Funeral Home on the West Side.

With the help of Phyllis Chesler (a gay homosexual herself and a writer who is also married to a divorce lawyer), Mom was able to find a gay rabbi. Unfortunately, there just aren't that many gay female rabbis in Manhattan. The one Mom found looked just like the insane love child of Jerry Garcia and Sandra Day O'Connor with a little bit of Primo Levi thrown in; personally I thought she was hot, but I'm not gay, or at least I think I'm not gay (please see forthcoming memoir entitled *Am I Gay or Not? The Life of Molly Jong-Fast*). Anyway, the gay homosexual rabbi wore a yarmulke over her bowl cut (please note that 45 percent of all optimistic lesbian rabbis have reported at one time in their lives having a bowl cut and dating a man who looked like Michael Bloomberg).

The problem was not so much how our optimistic rabbi looked but more how our optimistic rabbi sounded. She was long-winded. She was boring. She seemed uninterested in the funeral. She cleared her throat often. She had no idea whom she was burying and that seemed not to bother her and she kept doing this shtick that was very popular that year about life being a "journey" and death merely a "destination." Yeah, but it's a destination you're dead at.

Basically the problem with our optimistic rabbi was not

that she was an optimist or that she had a bowl cut but that she was a rabbi. Of course, she wasn't as bad as Rabbi Silverman of Greenwich (but then who is?), who buried my grandma Bette (see "I Caught the Bouquet at My Grandfather's Wedding") and who spent hours going on about his son's performance in *Weekend at Bernie's II.*

The funeral was a flop. Attendance was low. The service seemed unending. Various family members got into car accidents before and after (Hi, Timmy!). My friend Tanner came with me as my "date." He was best friends with the preppy murderer Robert Chambers in high school. He likes when I tell people that (Hi, Tanner!).

There was of course a silver lining; Grandma Eda thought it was a lovely wedding and wanted to know where we were going on our honeymoon. See, things had changed a bit with Grandma Eda. She had become very nice and very senile: the Mirsky nihilism had faded away when she began taking copious amounts of Prozac (hey, who doesn't?). In the vein of senility I told her Tanner and I were going to the Catskills (hey, why not). My bohemian grandma then told this bohemian story about the first time she ever met Grandpa in the very bohemian Catskills. "And I was an art teacher there and he was in the orchestra. It was the Depression and everyone was very, very poor and depressed; that's why they called it the Depression. We had to walk miles in the snow each day. And we couldn't afford shoes. And your grandfather liked to smoke tea and drink out of a flask. Speaking of which, is there some vodka for Grandma? Grandma would just love a little vodka. Oh, where was I? And one day he said to me,

'BABY WANNA PAINT MY DRUM?' (this is Mom's favorite line to repeat, again and again; please see *Fear of Fifty*) *and then we had sex on our first date in the woods.*" (Please note that the italicized section of this paragraph is a blatant libelous falsehood, or at least I wish it were a blatant libelous falsehood.)

And so, in the bohemian tradition of the Mirsky family, Grand-Aunt Kitty was put to rest and buried where all Jews are buried, in Queens near the airport.

Aunt Claudia, Aunt Nana, and Mom tossed dirt on Kitty's grave. So then did the other family members. Grandma wanted to know how we could have a Bat Mitzvah without swans made of chopped liver (Grandma loves chopped liver). My whole family was there, and my aunts, my cousins, and my platonic life friend Tanner. Everyone wore black, and everyone was blond and blue-eyed (except of course my Lebanese cousins, who really aren't blond). Kitty's much younger girlfriend didn't come to Kitty's funeral. Barbara Walters also did not come to Kitty's funeral (though of course she didn't know Kitty, she also didn't know Mom, and she also wasn't invited and she also was in L.A. with Tom Hanks talking about what it means to be a successful Hollywood parent).

Then we embarked on the eight-hour drive home. In the end I learned many important things from my Grand-Aunt Kitty. I learned that it's okay to be gay as long as you are also producing more Jews (though Kitty didn't end up producing more Jews). I learned that it's important to have children because otherwise you'll end up in a home. I learned that withholding your money from your children is the only way you can keep them from putting you in a home. I learned that being in a home is okay, if you can get pootie tang. I also learned the most important lesson of all: in the end everybody ends up several feet underground in Queens, near the airport.

i caught the bouquet at

my grandfather's wedding

❋

IN THE FIFTIES, my grandpa Howard Fast was a Communist who was jailed for refusing to name names to the House Un-American Activities Committee; five decades later he ended up in Greenwich, Connecticut. In the sixties, he sang with Pete Seeger at the Peekskill riots; four decades later he was Jeff Daniels's date to the A&E Awards ceremony. In his youth, he ran for Congress on the American Labor Party ticket; in his eighties he ran after his ten-year-old stepson. Once he was married to his causes; more recently he was married to his secretary.

Under her classic hats, beneath her shock of red hair, inside her pretty beige schmattes, my grandma Bette Fast was a true child of the Depression. Duty was the defining aspect of her life. When her country called on her during World War II, she drew cells for animated training films. When Dorothy Parker called on her, she held Dorothy's booze bottle out of sight. When Grandpa Howie went to jail, she took a job designing teen clothing. When anti-Communists threw rocks at her windows, she held her two young children tightly. When Grandpa Howie cheated on her with every famous actress west of the Mississippi, Grandma just kept baking sourdough bread. When Dashiell Hammett offered her an escape from all the chaos and philandering, she turned him down (of course Dashiell was a horrible drunk and probably wouldn't have been a better husband than Grandpa, but that's another story entirely).

Grandma's life revolved around Grandpa's foibles. Luckily Grandpa had many foibles to keep her busy. Grandpa wrote a novel a year. After Grandpa turned fifty, he got into this weird obsessive pattern. Every time Grandpa finished a novel, he told Bette it was time to move. Once a year Grandma would pack up all the beige leather sofas and all the tan rugs and move from one building to another on Fifth Avenue. She would set the new apartment up so it looked just like the old apartment. She would paint the new apartment the same color as the old apartment. She would use the same furniture, the same rugs, and the same art to re-create the previous apartment. So basically once a year Grandpa moved to a different building in a five-block radius. In fifteen years Grandpa and Grandma lived in almost every building on Fifth Avenue between Seventy-sixth and Eighty-third Streets.

Bette did her duty as the wife of a famous man, and was sort of rewarded with life on Fifth Avenue, two children and three grandchildren who adored her, hours of free time to sculpt, many beautiful beige dresses, and some degree of no-toriety. Unfortunately, she found doctors and hospitals un-chic, they offended her genteel sensibilities, and so she grew a tumor the size of a small quilted Chanel handbag with a tas-sel. All mildly amusing flipness aside, my grandma was the greatest woman I ever knew, and not a day goes by that I don't think about how much I miss and adore her.

After Grandma Bette died, life seemed bleak for my grandpa Howard Fast. Sure, he had authored more than eighty books (including *Spartacus, The Immigrants, Freedom Road,* and *April Morning*), won numerous prizes (among them the 1953 Stalin Peace Prize), and, as previously mentioned, spent some time in Mill Point Prison (1950) for refusing to name names in front of the House Un-American Activities Committee. Sure, the French loved him, the people of the Netherlands were always honoring him, and he still had some juice with the History Channel crowd. Sadly, his own people (the Jews, the readers of *The New York Review of Books*) felt Grandpa Howard had lived long enough. They felt it was time for him to move on to that Communist rally in the sky.

Grandpa did not agree. He preferred Woody Allen's take on immortality: "I don't want to achieve immortality through my work. I want to achieve it through not dying."

So Grandpa just kept on writing his usual book a year, as he had been doing for the last fifty years. Only now things had changed; sure, we weren't living on the moon or taking cars that flew in the sky, but Communism was no longer our enemy; in fact it was nowhere on the radar screen at all. The Cold War was over.

Communism had been replaced with a more heinous

threat—Islamic fundamentalists. Grandpa wasn't an Islamic fundamentalist, though he did enjoy the comic antics of one Jerry Lewis (ohh wait, that's the French). Because of his not being an Islamic fundamentalist (or possibly because of his incredible age, his huge body of work, and his refusal to die) his books basically stopped receiving publicity or even being reviewed. He became yet another sufferer of Herman Wouk syndrome. Herman Wouk syndrome is when everyone starts to associate you with dead people (people like everyone else in the Hollywood Ten, Richard Nixon, Sid Vicious, Margaret Thatcher, and Jesus), thus drawing the conclusion that you must be dead.

As an interesting and alarming sidebar, I will now insert a few lines from a poem the great Pablo Neruda wrote to my grandpa. It is by far Pablo Neruda's worst poem.

TO HOWARD FAST

I speak to you, Howard Fast. You, who are jailed.
I embrace you, my comrade; and I bid you good morning,
    my brother.

I am not of this country. I am from Chile.
My comrades are there, and my books and my house that
Gazes upon the cold Pacific's gigantic waves.

In these few lines, I think you get the point. Communism does not translate into good poetry, though it does translate into a good backdrop for James Bond movies.

The American people felt as if Grandpa had had a first act (Communism), a second (jail), a third (Greenwich), a fourth (more Greenwich), and two intermissions. It was time for him to die, so that his first editions would go up in value and *The New York Times* could run his obituary, which they had been keeping close at hand for the last three decades. After all, everyone else who'd been involved with the House Un-American Activities Committee was dead: Zero Mostel, John Howard Lawson, Alvah Bessie, Samuel Ornitz, Ring Lardner, Jr., Dalton Trumbo, and even Senator Joseph McCarthy.

Another sign of Herman Wouk syndrome is that, of the small amount of press you get, almost all is alarmingly positive. This positive publicity was produced by a thin stream of film crews from France and the Netherlands. It would go down like this—two mustached foreigners would arrive armed with only basic English, one camera, an old Volvo station wagon, and the knowledge that the average American man doesn't live much past eighty. They would then make themselves comfortable, helping themselves to prune juice and the other earthly delights available at Grandpa's house, such as FiberCon wafers and bran chips. Then they would sit on the beige leather sofa that Grandpa had owned since McCarthy was just a junior senator. The emphasis of these interviews always shifted from a particular project to lifetime achievements. Hans and Blix (most of the cameramen were not named Hans and Blix, but what if they were?) would then look at Grandpa as if he were a large taxidermied dodo bird. They would watch him smoke his small, thin cigars and listen to him ramble on about Communism.

"So," Hans would say as he fumbled with his tape recorder, "tell us about your feelings about the current administration's policy on Cuba."

Grandpa would then light up (both his face and his ci-gars) and start bitching about how stupid other people were. Sometimes Grandpa would get facts wrong. And sometimes Grandpa would just lie.

Basically, these camera crews served as good grandchil-dren (thank you, Hans; thank you, Blix). Hans and Blix never noticed if Grandpa lied or got things wrong. All Herman Wouk syndrome aside, if a camera crew comes to you to ask you about your "lifetime" anything, it's because they think your lifetime is just about to end.

Since he wasn't, contrary to popular belief, dead, How-ard Fast had no choice but to go on living. He had to em-brace life, so he did what any rich, single octogenarian would do—he married his secretary, a plucky young southern belle from New Orleans, who was one half Tammy Faye Bakker and one half Laura Bush.

Now I'm not greedy. Okay, I am greedy, really greedy, and moneygrubbing, too. And vain and shallow, and some-what self-obsessed, and depressed, and catty, and alarmingly materialistic, and often crass and lazy, and I would have cheated on my SATs—if someone had shown me how. But that said, I had some high hopes for Grandpa's will. I mean, sure, I understood I was gonna have to share. I understood that my dad and aunt would have to split everything, but I thought I would do okay. I thought my dad would surely cut me in for a third of his half when he died. Unfortunately, he's a vegetarian, so he could live a long, long time, but I was willing to wait.

But all this thinking happened before I saw Grandpa's new, young wife to be and her three children. Upon first meeting them, I realized Grandpa wasn't the only one getting screwed. Luckily, I knew a little algebra. I calculated the famed Anna Nicole Smith formula (initial inheritance − difference between bride's and groom's ages × ten ≠ what you would have gotten if Grammy hadn't died)—when the bride is half the groom's age and has three children, the chances of the wayward ex-junkie granddaughter (me) inheriting Tara become quite slim.

The blessed union was held at Grandpa's house in Old Greenwich, Connecticut. Old Greenwich is a flat, cheerless suburb with half-acre zoning, where the upper-middle-class people who work for the upper-class people who live in Greenwich live. So, for example, the well-paid florist or the successful pool man or the local Communist might live in Old Greenwich. Since Grandma's untimely demise, Grandpa had hightailed it off Lake Avenue in backcountry real-money Greenwich as fast as you can say "assisted suicide." This is just a joke, of course; Grandpa didn't kill Grandma. Grandpa moved to Old Greenwich because it was cheaper, and he likes cheaper things because he is . . . cheap.

It was a small shotgun wedding attended by the Belle's three sons, the sons' twenty-seven friends, my two little brothers, myself, my dad, my stepmom, my aunt, my uncle, Sterling Lord (my grandpa's agent), and a bunch of other old people in wheelchairs whom I had never met before but who looked olde with an e.

Of course Grandpa wasn't olde with an e. He was only 83 on his wedding day. He had at least another twenty or thirty good solid years with his Belle. Of course he did have congestive heart failure, emphysema, a series of recurring small strokes affecting the nervous column, coronary artery disease, the beginnings of Alzheimer's, and a bad case of dementia, but other than that there was no reason why he couldn't live to be 113 years old.

But back to the blessed union: it took place in the living room of Grandpa's house. The leather sofa was pushed against the wall. The air was thick with the aroma of musty furniture. White paper flowers were hung from the walls, candles were lit, and crazy Cousin Lenny started playing the piano.

It's important here to add that I did not dislike my step-grandmother because she was a substantially smarter and weirder and shorter and flatter-chested and less blond and more sober version of Anna Nicole Smith. I did not dislike my new stepgrandmother because her sons were out shooting squirrels and drinking beer on the lawn during the services, okay, maybe they weren't, but you know they were thinking of it. I did not dislike my new stepgrandmother because she was from the place where *The Dukes of Hazzard* was created. I did not dislike my new stepgrammy because she offended my limousine-liberal-Upper-West-Side-Jewish-Gore-loving-Ben-Shahn-owning-socialist-summer-camp-going sensibilities. I disliked my new stepgrammy because I missed my real grandmother, who had died two years before of stomach cancer (see, I'm deep and sensitive).

Let me just add one other possible explanation for why I didn't love my stepgrammy. She looked like a Republican. She had that head of Republican helmet hair, the kind that never loses shape. She had that thick, glossy Republican skin. She had a small cluster of brown Republican freckles around her nose. She even wore smart Republican pantsuits made in the USA of synthetic fabrics. Of course she wasn't a Republican (let's give Grandpa a little credit here). But isn't having the fashion sense of a Washington, D.C./southern Republican just as bad as being one?

The wedding was quick. The bride wore a white suit. The groom wore Depends. I walked around the small, dark house making a mental inventory of everything that would someday be inventoried in Grandpa's last will and testament. I seriously considered stealing the schlocky Norman Rockwell that Norman made for grandfather because both Norman and Grandpa were loved by the *Reader's Digest* crowd or possibly because both Norman and Grandpa mined the American Revolution like it was their battle with bulimia or possibly Norman made the painting for Grandpa because he was secretly in love with Grandpa and he wasn't the ear-cutting-off type. Or most possible of all, Norman Rockwell was a Commie, a red. Just kidding, Rockwell estate, you don't have to be a Communist to love and want to have anal sex with my grandpa. You just have to be gay, and clearly Norman Rockwell was a gay homosexual.

Think of Norman's famous "prom dress" *Saturday Evening Post* cover from March 19, 1949. The painting shows a young girl in jeans and a plaid work shirt standing in front of a mirror holding a white prom dress in front of her. The young girl is beautiful, innocent. Her hair is pinned up. This is clearly a self-portrait. Obviously, Norman Rockwell sees himself as a beautiful girl. He sees Communism as an exquisite white prom dress. Beyond doubt, Norman is painting himself in this painting. The girl's white bobby sox are just the kind Norman used to wear around the house when he dressed up like Grace Kelly and did the bunny hop. The jeans and work shirt represent Norman's American, boring, heterosexual life. The prom dress is his real self, Communism.

But I didn't steal the painting or anything else because I'm no Winona Ryder, I'm much fatter than she is, and besides (the real reason) it was at that time very hard to unload a Norman Rockwell, stolen or not. During the mid-nineties Rockwell was *out,* and I don't mean of the closet.

My adorable little brothers, both of whom I am madly in love with, seemed confused as to why my aunt and father were so upset. Ben, the elder of the two, who was at the time fourteen (who is now single and so handsome and brilliant and a National Merit scholar and goes to Princeton—his e-mail is bfast@princeton.edu, and he's half-Jewish too), was happy for Grandpa, though a little disconcerted by the fact that he had a ten-year-old uncle. Danny, the younger of the two (who is also brilliant and handsome and now, just a few years later, rows crew and plays the viola), asked again, "Why are Daddy and Auntie Rachel crying?"

I took Danny into the other room and explained to him, "Sometimes when a child has a parent who makes them crazy, a parent who antagonizes them, they need to look to the future to find comfort." Danny and I were sitting on Grandpa's bed in his dark bedroom in Old Greenwich. Outside we saw stretches of flat houses and miles of golf course; inside we saw stretches of having a stepgrammy younger than Dad and three uncles whose names rhymed (Dusty, Rusty, and Lusty).

"Sis? I have no idea what you're talking about. Are you back on the drugs?"

Ha, kids say the darnedest things! But I wasn't back on the drugs. The whole world was on drugs! Danny didn't understand. He'd grown up in the wilds of Cos Cob (a neighboring suburb) and was only ten. If Danny had grown up in New York City, he'd already have five beepers and would be getting Botox shot into his forehead on a regular basis.

As the minister (or justice of the peace or rabbi or whatever) said, "I now pronounce you husband and wife," the scene somehow became clear to me. Sure, we were an odd, madcap family filled with odd madcaps, sure Grandpa had been in jail and my mom was very pregnant when she married my dad, but we weren't the kind of family who engaged in this kind of thing. Wait, actually, now that I think about it, we were exactly the kind of family who engaged in this kind of thing. Maybe it was the visual of my octogenarian of a grandpa and his nubile youngish secretary that finally convinced me my family wasn't exactly, um, normal.

After the pronouncement, everyone who'd been featured in Grandpa's pre-Belle will found himself or herself inconsolable. The Belle's three sons ran around trying to find the keg they had bought for the occasion, and someone tripped on one of my dead grandmother's huge bronze sculptures and almost broke his ankle. Vivacious, voluptuous Cousin Debbie kept trying to hug me. My grandma's old nurse got wasted on Wild Turkey and passed out in the bushes. And Godzuki, my black-and-white cocker spaniel, squatted down, pressed her little black doggy lips into a smile, and peed on the white shag rug in the hall.

And then, as soon as it had started, it was over. All of a sudden I had a ten-year-old uncle and a grandmother who was three years older than my boyfriend. As quickly as Grandpa had lost the prenuptial agreement, which he said he had signed but then couldn't find, as quickly as the Belle had moved in and removed all the photos of my grandma, as quickly as Hong Kong went back to China, Grandpa was married to his southern Belle.

Great cheers came from the Belle, her three sons, the Belle's elderly mother (who was still younger than Grandpa), and the sons' twenty-seven friends, who'd already set half the backyard on fire trying to roast a stray injured pigeon. The groom wobbled over and kissed the bride. I shielded Danny's eyes (I figured it was my responsibility to cut future therapy bills wherever I could). The cork was popped on a bottle of champagne. In the grand Fast tradition, people started to drink and continued to cry. Someone started playing "Send in the Clowns" on the out-of-tune piano. Then the bride, who was standing in the middle of the living room, bouquet in one hand, cigarette in the other, started jumping up and down, screaming: "I got him! I got him!"

I leaned over to my aunt Rachel, who was both drinking and crying, who is the skinniest woman in the entire world and looks like Bette Davis and once dated both Philip Roth and Ken Burrows, who is now my stepfather and has been married to my mother for a staggering eleven years. I leaned over to her and said, "She didn't just say that, right?"

"It must be a southern thing?"

"No?" We looked at each other. "The South can't possibly be that weird, can it? I mean, after all, it's just the South, it's not Mars."

Before we could really ponder these things, it was time to begin the crucial reform ritual of butchering all the Jewish wedding traditions. And so we blundered blindly through Havah Nagilah, the circle dancing, the chair-bouncing dance (think of frail old Grandpa being tossed up and down on a rickety folding chair by my three blond-haired, Aryan "uncles," who don't know what a bialy is), the Di Di Anu, and the glass breaking.

As my new uncles (who ranged in age between ten and twenty-one) drank beer and tortured the family dog in the garden, it was immediately clear to me that this group would somehow *not* form a family. See, Grandma Bette was beautiful, sensitive, smart, and tasteful, and she was all about a certain German Jewish sensibility. Of course I come from a family of Polish Jews, and everyone knows that Polish Jews are lowest on the class totem pole. Polish Jews are lower than German Jews, lower than Russian Jews, lower than Ukrainian Jews, lower than British Jews, lower than Portuguese or Bolivian Jews. Polish Jews weren't even in steerage, they had to swim behind the ship. The only people we're better than are the Hungarian Jews. Because, as they say—"Polish Jews and Hungarian Jews will sell you their mothers, but only Hungarian Jews will deliver." I, of course, would sell you my mother, but . . .

But that said, let's not oversimplify the Belle. She was much more than just wine in a box and "yee-haws." The Belle was also one of those people who kept sabotaging her own life by accident. The Belle was a professional victim: her husband left her, money was stolen from her, friends deserted her, and the Chicago Merc stole her idea for the commodities exchange (this I have some trouble believing). I doubt she married Grandpa for money; more likely, she married him for the devastation and drama of his dying just a few years later.

Also, I personally didn't like the Belle because she just wouldn't stop talking (which in our family is my job).

But back to the wedding: All of a sudden my ears perked up as I heard my calling—"Would all the single women get on the dance floor?" (the floor of my grandpa's living room). I knew what was coming. I knew there was only one reason for all the single women to stand in the middle of the room. I knew there was only one thing that could happen at that moment . . . unless—a hopeful thought came springing into my dry and barren brain—maybe they were going to shoot us.

No such luck. Now, I love trying to catch the bouquet because I love superstition, competition, and any ritual that shames. There's nothing that makes me feel better about myself than getting up in the middle of the room and showing everyone that I am still single, that I have not yet been able to trick some dim-witted banker into marrying me. This particular bouquet toss was especially touching, because the other single women were in wheelchairs and most did not have their original teeth. Actually, that's not true. My grandfather's housekeeper, who spoke only Slovenian, did have all her own teeth, but she had been married before. So I crossed her palm with ten dollars (I would have given her more, but as I think I mentioned earlier I'm cheap), and she was so moved by my outpouring of money that she promised me she wouldn't go for the bouquet.

Suddenly I found myself surrounded by angry octogenarians. My grandpa's young wife looked at me and smiled. I wondered if she was going to toss me the bouquet as her way of apologizing for all the inheritance she was going to squander. A ninety-five-year-old grandcousin of mine "accidentally" ran over my foot. One of Grandpa's old Commie gals with a walker plowed into my left side; she apologized, offering the weak excuse of not being able to see. The Belle's mother (a widow) parked her wheelchair right between her daughter and me. I was able to unlock her little wheelchair brake, and trust me, she moved.

Someone from the crowd yelled out drunkenly, "Just throw the f—ing bouquet already." The Belle screamed "Yeehaw" and tossed the bouquet directly at me. It hit me on the head and bounced off. Luckily, I recovered swiftly, though I still can't see out of my left eye (okay, I'm lying). All of a sudden I was struck with emotion, or ptomaine from the supermarket sushi I'd eaten earlier in the car. It was then that I realized I too wanted to be married. At that moment I realized I could marry anyone I wanted to. I could marry a Bolivian Jew or a Tibetan guru. I could marry a goy or a man named Roy. I could marry a sex offender or a person who works for the magazine *Blender*. I could marry a man with an unfortunate orange tan. I could marry a shrink or a man who owned an ice rink. I could even marry a serial killer or a man who drank Miller or a person who was close friends with Ben Stiller.

I wanted a huge wedding, not some bohemian shindig in the living room (as is par for the course in my family). I wanted ice sculptures, swans made of chopped liver, cookies made in the likeness of my betrothed and myself. And of course no tasteful wedding would be complete without a dessert bar, a sushi bar, and a caviar bar. I wanted my name on two hundred boxes of pastel pink Jordan almonds. I wanted a cake that cost more than a liver transplant. I wanted a wedding website. I wanted to have my picture in the Style Section. And above all, I wanted to register.

At that moment I realized that I may be the granddaughter of a Communist and the daughter of a feminist, but deep down I'm all capitalist. In that very second I saw that weddings were about more than just love, friends, and family. Weddings were about presents, they were about impressing other people, they were about excluding people whom I resented, and most important, weddings were about showing off. So I smiled flirtatiously at the oldest of my uncles, I showed a bit of thigh to my cousin Lenny, I raised the bouquet over my head triumphantly and screamed, "I'm twenty years old and I'm next! Watch out, world! I'm next!"

heavenly hash

٭

AS A CHILD I liked many things: doughnuts, French toast, pancakes, cookies, brownies, chocolate cake, vanilla cake, all flavors of frosting, Ring Dings, Ding Dongs, yellow Hostess cupcakes, chocolate Hostess cupcakes, Ho Ho's, pasta, chocolate, and marzipan. I even liked chopped liver. The problem was that I didn't much like anything else. I hated reading. I hated the outdoors. I pretty much hated other children. I hated playing. I kind of even hated our dog. I liked TV, though. I also liked presents.

This dislike of so many things caught my mother's attention. It upset her. She consulted my many shrinks. They spoke earnestly to her about my many problems. Personally, I now think that hatred of all things is hardly a problem, and honestly I'd still rather watch TV, eat, and get presents than do anything else. See, the shrinks thought I was sick. My

mom thought I was troubled. My nanny thought I was depressed. But the truth was, I was just smart.

Looking back, I am prouder of my love of these things
than if I'd been a child prodigy, because the truth was I *was* a
child prodigy. Even at ten I knew what it takes most people
their whole lives to figure out: that TV, food, and presents are
the best things in the world.

So my many earnest shrinks and my mother decided that
my total apathy about life wasn't a good thing. They decided
I needed something to show me how to love again. But what
could teach me to love again? Maybe a huge TV could teach
me to love again, or perhaps a giant Hershey's Kiss? Nope,
that's not what they had in mind. Now that is not to say I was
heading for shock treatment. My many shrinks and my mom
had decided I needed a hobby (preferably something ath-
letic), and that hobby was to be of my choosing. It could be
anything: French lessons (ha), ice-skating lessons (gag me,
please), tennis lessons (real Jewish), anything. But you see,
I knew right away what I wanted for my hobby. I wanted
something that I could do while sitting down, something re-
laxing, something that didn't take too much time. I wanted
the laziest sport I could think of, and since I didn't know
what golf was, I opted for horseback riding.

Ahh, horseback riding. I took my first lesson and I was
hooked. I loved it. I loved the horses. I loved the way they
smelled. I loved their long, flowing hair. I loved everything
about riding. I loved the outfits. I loved the gear. I loved the
way the girls at the stables got me Snickers bars with my
lunch. I loved everything about riding. Except the riding.

Well, that's not entirely true. At first I loved the riding. I

was fearless (or as fearless as a fear-ridden, completely neurotic, violently anxious Jewish girl could be). At first I was
well-behaved and happy. They put me on this sixteen-year-
old horse named Hank. Now a sixteen-year-old horse is the
horse equivalent of Strom Thurmond except without the
remarks about how great the Confederacy was. Hank was
brown, but his muzzle had become gray from age. Hank was
very tall, about seventeen hands high. Hank was also half-
dead and thus excellent for me to ride. I would get on Hank
in my purple T-shirt and my purple riding hat, and we would
wobble around the ring. He was really on his last legs. If
Hank were a human he'd have been wearing diapers. You
knew he'd never take off and gallop away because, quite
frankly, that kind of activity would have killed him. Hank was
a wonderful horse. Unfortunately, one day he died and I had
to find some other horse to ride.

Meanwhile, back on the Upper East Side of Manhattan,
Mom and the many therapists were incredibly thrilled with
my having found something I liked to do besides eating. They
were impressed. They were very, very impressed. Mom was so
gleeful about my having found this other activity that she
bought me a pony. Of course I had to nag her for the pony, as
all little kids do. I had to sit on one of the chairs that we called
elephant testicles (because that's what they looked like) in
her huge office in the town house with the hot pink door and
say, "Mooooooooom, plllllllllllllllllease can I have a pony? Pllllllllllllease. Plllllllllllllllllllllllllllllllllllllllllllleaaaaaaaaaaaase. Pllllll-
lllllllllllllllllllllllllllllllllleeeeeeeeeeeeeeeeeaaaaaaaaaaaaaaaaaasssssssee!
I need a pony; come on, Mommy."

And then she smiled, with the knowledge that I had

found something I liked to do. Then she said, "No, I think it's too expensive."

That prompted me to scream and cry. I screamed and cried and cried and screamed. Then I told Mom, "You're a bad bad bad mom. I hate you. I hate you so so so so so so so so so so so so so much! But I'd love you if you got me a pony."

Then she said: "You can hate me, but I'm not getting you a pony."

But I knew something about Mom that even Mom didn't know. I knew that Mom had a very low tolerance for being nagged. I knew that Mom was like a majestic oak tree and I was like the Charmin company. The majestic oak tree would put up a fight. She would not want to be made into toilet paper. She'd give the great big saw a hard time. But in the end, she, like everyone else in this crazy, crazy world, would fall and end up as toilet paper.

So I put the plan into action; I cried and screamed for three days and three nights (like the forty days and forty nights of flooding), and at the end of those days and nights Mom said, "Okay, I'll get you a f—ing pony."

And so it was that I gratefully accepted Mom's generous offer.

Of course we still had to find the pony. Now, I really hadn't ridden any horses but the half-dead horse, so let's just say I was in for a slight surprise. I just didn't know that there were horses out there that weren't half-dead, that didn't only go from walk to trot and back again.

Over the next few weeks I rode lots and lots of horses.

Did I mention that I wasn't a good rider? Well, I wasn't a good rider. I was a really bad rider. Which means that during those few weeks while I was auditioning horses, I was really just falling off horses. The first week I rode a black mare who tossed me on a fence. The next week I rode a gray gelding who nearly bucked me off. The next week I rode a roan gelding who shied from a car backfire and went flying. I had my foot caught in the stirrup, so I got dragged around the ring, not quite unconscious, with my head bouncing up and down.

Now I try to limit my self-destructive impulses to things that I know can't hurt me. You see, I am always first and foremost a Jewish neurotic. I like self-destructive behavior that is along the lines of not wearing a seat belt in a taxi. I was getting the idea from all this falling that possibly this could be a somewhat dangerous sport. And the incident with the roan gelding had really scared me; after all, I had gotten into riding because of the sitting aspect of the sport, and I wasn't doing a whole lot of sitting. Besides which, the roan gelding fall had caused the following incident:

After they caught the roan gelding and removed me from the stirrup that was connected to the horse's saddle, which was of course attached to the horse's back, the stables called my mom. They had a bleed policy, which meant if you were bleeding they'd call your parents. This was not the first time my parents had been called. I was still slightly stunned, sitting in a chair in the stable. It was summer. The horse had been put back in his box. He was fine, pleased to have shown another little kid with a whip who was boss.

I was a little shaken. Mom came to the stable right away. "Ohhhhhh, my God! My baby." Then Mom started crying when she saw me, which was sort of puzzling.

"Can I get a Snickers bar on the way to the doctor's?" My arm was gushing blood. Mom held the towel to my arm tightly.

"Oh baby, Mommy's gonna make it all better."

"Can I get a Snickers bar on the way?"

"Oh, do you need a hug, baby?"

"Can we stop at Peter's Market and get a Snickers bar on the way to the doctor's?"

"Oh, darling," Mom said, and started crying. It didn't take much to get Mom crying.

"Can I get that Snickers bar?"

"Oh, baby, baby, baby. Mommy loves you so much."

Mom got me a Snickers bar on the way to the doctor's. When we got to the doctor's office, the doctor saw me first, either because I was bleeding or because my mom was Erica Jong.

By the mid-eighties, we no longer lived in Weston (unless of course you are the IRS, in which case we still live in Weston), we only spent the weekends in Weston (Weston is the tiny town with just a gas station and a liquor store right next to Westport). But I knew the Weston-Westport area well enough to know that I didn't like the local pediatrician. The pediatrician's office was in the town of Westport, right behind the movie theater, near the giant Gap store, and the even gianter Banana Republic. Westport is a sort of low-rent Greenwich populated by Jews and Paul Newman. The doctor's office was sort of standard, but since it was a pediatrician's office there were obnoxious posters of kittens everywhere. This pediatrician had seen me when I was a little kid (when we lived in Westport full-time) and saw me only when I was bleeding from one of my many accidents (like falling off a horse or tripping and having my pinkie chopped off by a shard of plate).

"Ohh, that looks okay," the female pediatrician said, while feeling my arm. "So, Erica, are you working on something new? I loved you on *Donahue* the other day. You were amazing!"

"Well, actually I'm working on a novel about Venice."

"Oh, I love Venice. It's so romantic. Who doesn't love Venice?" Evil pediatrician woman made a grand gesture with her hands to show that everyone loves Venice. "That's a fantastic idea for a novel. When is it coming out?"

"It should come out in about eleven months."

"Ohh, I'm sorry, am I bothering anyone here? Don't mind me, I'm bleeding to death."

The pediatrician smiled. "Bleeding to death? No, you're going to be just fine. I'm just going to give you a little tetanus shot, then bandage this sucker right up and we'll be in business."

"You didn't say tetanus shot, did you?"

The pediatrician laughed. Mom laughed. "This won't hurt at all." The pediatrician smiled as she got out a huge needle, stuck it into a tiny jar, and filled it with an evil-looking fluid.

"You know what?"

"What?" the pediatrician asked.

"That looks like it's gonna hurt a lot."

"Well it's not. By the way, Erica, do you think you'd mind looking at this script my nephew wrote? It's really good. I think you might really enjoy it. It's all about Club Med."

"Well, let's just say I'm not gonna stick around to find out whether sticking that enormous needle in my arm is going to hurt." And I ran out the door to the pediatrician's office, through her very crowded waiting room, and into the street. Both Mom and the pediatrician went after me. I didn't get very far, I only got to the parking lot before the pediatrician caught me, smiled a horrible, jagged-toothed smile, and said, "You don't want to scare the other patients now, do you?"

Of course my great escape was futile, and it ended with Mom making me write "I will not make a public scene" one hundred times on a pad of legal paper. Luckily, Mom felt bad and ended up making me write it only fifty times.

I really didn't like having that shot. I really liked the Snickers bar. I even liked the car ride to the doctor's. But I really didn't want to ever have another shot. So in the back of my mind I decided I might just kind of cool it on the riding. The only problem with that was my mom was preparing to buy me a pony and I couldn't just change my mind. After all, I had nagged for this pony. I had begged for this pony. I had whined for this pony. I had kvetched for this pony. I had even gone on a ten-minute hunger strike for this pony. I had worked for this pony, and on principle I wasn't going to give up now; in many ways I was like Richard Gere and his selfless quest to free Tibet, or perhaps I was like the young PETA-supporting starlet who is true to her cause until she is tapped to model Gucci's fur line, or maybe I was like a young Jane Fonda. I had beliefs, damn it. They were beliefs I was willing to kvetch for, to nag for, to guilt-trip for.

And so I continued auditioning ponies, until one day a pony came into my life that I knew was so fat and so old that he'd never have the strength to toss me off. This pony truly was on his last legs. This pony really looked like he was en route to the glue factory. This pony could have been named Elmer. This was the pony for me. After all, I thought, how long can this guy have left? A few months tops.

Mom was happy that I was still riding. She was of course worried that I would die, but she was also proud of me for not quitting. Mom had this big thing about not being a quitter. I loved quitting. I'd quit almost everything I'd ever done. I left every summer camp early. I left every school after a few years. My motto was, "Why stress when you can give up?" But that said, Mom was proud of her little girl for sticking to it.

Personally I was just happy I'd found a horse that didn't have that much longer to go. I figured I'd ride Heavenly Hash around a few times and then he'd die and I'd pretend to be so traumatized from him dying that I'd never ride again.

Now it's important here to mention that at the stable the worst thing you could do was quit because of a fall. It was considered cowardly and uncool. Never one to be uncool, I knew I had to enact plan B. Basically I knew I had to wait around for Heavenly Hash to kick it. After all, the respect of the drugged-up blond-haired sixteen-year-old horse groupies was all I had in this world (that and my love of food and my numerous toys).

And so I set off on plan B. Mom bought me Heavenly

Hash. Heavenly Hash was the perfect pony for me because he was exactly like me. We were both nervous, fat, and depressed. Sure, he had gray hair and I had red hair. Sure, he was a pony and I was a human. Sure, he ate the wood his stall was made of, and I ate delicious chocolate-covered doughnuts. Sure, he was ridden with a crop and I went to the Dalton School until I was kicked out (there's really no way they're gonna let my son, Max, in now). Sure, he went lame and I went to a shrink who looked at me earnestly and asked me how I felt about things. But the truth was, me and my pony, we were basically the same.

Right before buying Heavenly Hash, Mom had the following conversation with his owner:

"So Heavenly Hash is a good pony?" Mom asked.

"A good pony?" the large, mustached owner said. "He's a great pony. He's the best pony. He's a push-button pony."

"What the hell does that mean?" Mom asked.

"A push-button pony is so easy to ride it's like pushing a button. You push a button and then he goes, like a machine. Except he's not a machine, he's a pony. He's a push-button pony." The whole conversation felt like it came right out of a Coen brothers movie.

So Mom bought Heavenly Hash, and I set about not riding him. After all, I was no dummy. I'd had shots. I'd had to go to the dreaded doctor. I had learned my lesson. I was ready to not ride that pony. Unfortunately, the girls at the stable noticed I wasn't riding my pony, and they made me ride the pony.

So once a week, I'd come down to the Weston Equestrian Center (which is now condos) and timidly mount my flea-bitten gray (even his color was a bad sign) pony. I would then ride him around the ring approximately once and bring him back to his stall and let him hang out and crib (that's when the horse is so nervous that it eats the wood that its stall is made of).

My plan was working great. I'd gone almost two whole weeks without being injured. I was truly impressed with my problem-solving ability. So one Sunday I was in the indoor ring with the Elvis of ponies, Heavenly Hash. We were just cruising around, doing a little trotting, nothing major, nothing that could have gotten Heavenly Hash's pacemaker going, when all of a sudden the one stallion in the barn broke off his crossties and came running into our ring. Now, Heavenly Hash was a gelding. Needless to say, he wasn't so nuts about those stallions, and the stallion wasn't so nuts about anyone.

Heavenly Hash started bucking. I was shocked, because I had gotten him with the understanding that he was half-dead. I grabbed his neck and held on for my life. That minute was the closest I will ever come to being Jewel's rodeo-riding boyfriend, and I thank God for that, truly I do. I held on tight, all the while screaming, "I'm gonna die." Now, interestingly enough, this is not so different from being on a plane with me.

Sooner or later one of the stoned blond teenage girls who worked at the stable (whom I liked because she gave me Snickers bars) came by and grabbed the stallion. Then she smiled at me and said something to the effect of "I hope that didn't disturb your ride."

I smiled, and tried not to look like a neurotic Jewish wreck. "Ohh, no, I was just about to go jump some huge water jump."

"Cool, cool," she said and wandered off.

See, there was one fundamental difference between the other riders out there and me. They were not scared of horses. They were not scared of falling. They were not scared of riding. They were not me. After I put Heavenly Hash back in his box that day, I realized that I really could live my life to good purpose and never ride again. I wanted a new hobby, something that didn't involve staring death in the face every time I did it. Okay, maybe I wasn't staring death in face, but just the reality of staring another tetanus shot in the face was enough for me to stop.

There was of course only one problem. Mom had bought me a pony and she kind of expected me to ride it. So I had to get creative (or get chicken pox). First I got the flu, then a head cold, then I got diphtheria (or I convinced the adults around me I had it). I was heading toward mono when Mom asked me if there was something wrong.

And meanwhile at the stable, good old Heavenly Hash wasn't faring all that well either (except that he wasn't faking it and I was). First he'd gotten something in his shoe. This something had caused him to become horribly lame. This lameness led to increased nervousness and increased cribbing, which led to Heavenly Hash getting a blockage, which led to endless jokes by my mother about giant horse suppositories. Heavenly Hash was in trouble. All the vets in the world couldn't save Heavenly Hash; it was love he needed. The love of a little girl; that would bring him back to health.

So of course we did what any caring person would have done in that situation: we sold the money hemorrhager (after all, there's room for only one of those in my family). For just a fourth of the price Mom bought him for, Heavenly Hash was heading to a better place: the glue factory. Heavenly Hash was heading for greener pastures, otherwise known as the inside of a bottle of Elmer's glue. And so, after a few short months of being owned by me, Heavenly Hash belonged to the world.

Mom was pretty mad about the whole thing. She didn't like buying a pony and then selling it for a huge loss. She didn't like the fact that I hadn't been riding the pony. She was annoyed with the many earnest shrinks for their expensive suggestion. She didn't like having paid for suppositories for the last few months. She didn't like Heavenly Hash, and quite frankly, she wasn't so nuts about me. After all, if I'd just come clean about not wanting to ride anymore, then she could have saved quite a lot of money, money that could have gone to helping homeless children or perhaps to shopping. Personally, I was just thrilled that I had lived through the whole debacle. I was ready to re-devote my life to avoiding pain or injury. I was ready to start some piano lessons.

Ultimately I learned many, many things from my experience of owning a pony. I learned that ponies are expensive. I learned that parents can easily be driven to the point of wanting to give you up for adoption. I learned that all children want ponies, but almost no children should be given ponies. I learned that parents don't like to throw away money. I learned that all children love ponies, but not all ponies love children. I also learned that sometimes you have to kill a pony so that said pony can go and be with Jesus.

In the end Heavenly Hash didn't go to the glue factory. Yes, Heavenly Hash had a second act. He had a career longer than that of Heart or Kris Kross or Vanilla Ice, though Heavenly Hash probably would have preferred to pack it in and head to the riding rink in the sky. Sometimes I think I see Heavenly Hash wandering the streets, lost, looking for the girl who owned him for exactly three months—longer than many Hollywood marriages, but still. Then I realize that's not Heavenly Hash wandering the streets looking for me, it's a certain freebie-obsessed daytime talk-show host who lives in my neighborhood and bears an uncanny resemblance to my childhood pony. When I look at this daytime talk-show host in her free Gucci sunglasses and her free Coach leather coat and her free Citizens of Humanity jeans, I realize that sometimes getting what you want (a pony) isn't the most important thing in life. Sometimes the best things in life are free, even if you have to steal them.

how to get famous without

really trying

※

SOMETHING ABOUT my pony-loving past makes me think quite a lot about the ill-fated union of Benjamin Affleck and the great Jennifer Lopez and in turn just how difficult it is to be famous. There's the constant badgering by photographers, the need to stay razor thin, the unrelenting stress about image, the adoration of millions, the shopping, the free stuff, the being treated better than the pope, the flying first class, and who could forget that nasty *National Enquirer*. But the really tough thing about being famous is the legions of servants.

Fame is expensive. Luckily famous people are like giant, thin, tan, surgically altered oak trees whose leaves are hundred-dollar bills. Famous people make a *lot* of money. Of course there's a problem with making a lot of money: if you're not used to a lot of money, you tend to spend a lot of money (I believe this is called "Hammer Time").

Now there are lots and lots and lots and lots of people (writers or not) who are more famous than my mom is: Stephen King, Danielle Steel, Jackie Collins, Phil Collins, Joan Lunden, and Paris Hilton. But they are not related to me. So I will need to illustrate my thesis by providing examples from the life of my mother, one Erica Mann Jong.

The first employee you need when you are famous is a secretary. This is because *no* famous person makes her own phone calls. If you make your own phone calls, you are simply not famous. That is because when you get famous it becomes very hard to dial numbers: your fingers become very weak and your hand-eye coordination goes out the window. Also, as a famous person you forget how to type or use a copier, a fax machine, or a checkbook, and this is where you get into trouble.

The first secretary I remember we will call Tippi Hedren. While this secretary was neither "Tippi" nor "Hedren," she was rather dippy when it came to certain secretarial skills. And though she was neither American nor the star of *The Birds,* we will call her Tippi Hedren anyway so she doesn't sue my punk Jewish ass. Tippi Hedren bred and trained doggies—in the interest of specificity, schnauzers. Tippi was British. She thought I was fat (that was the general consensus), though she still supplied me with ample amounts of shortbread. I love shortbread, though not as much as I love large bars of colored chocolate (please see chapter relating to Venice for colored chocolate). Tippi had short, gray hair and a clipped British accent. She seemed as if she was always slightly annoyed. Tippi was nippy.

We lived in rural, poverty-stricken Weston, Connecticut, where all the kids wore J. Crew and drove around in Jeep Grand Cherokees and listened to the music of P. Diddy or, as he was called all those many years ago, Puff Daddy. Tippi worked in a small, windowless closet near Mom's office. The closet was closed off from the rest of the house by sliding glass doors, which one could lock. Tippi liked the closet because it reminded her for some reason of boarding school. Tippi was a tad trippy.

In her spare time Tippi wrote wildly successful books on dog breeding, the kind that she still gets royalty checks from. Eventually Tippi decided she didn't really need this aggravation (after all, she was making four times the amount of money I'll ever make. Doesn't that make you feel bad for me? I feel bad for me. Or maybe you might want to drop me a small piece of fan mail, nothing major, a present perhaps), and she quit. In the end Tippi was with Mom for about five years, which is actually a record when it comes to celebrity employment. Gwyneth Paltrow has a British assistant, which makes me wonder if Mom and Gwyneth Paltrow are actually the same person. Think about it, have you ever seen them together?

Next came a secretary whom I will call Ricky Martin. I would just like to reiterate that like her predecessor, Tippi Hedren, this secretary was not actually *the* Ricky Martin, nor was she even named Ricky or Martin. She wasn't even Hispanic, she was Italian (or she might have just been Jewish) and lived on Staten Island. But that is really not the point; the point is that for this essay we will call Mom's secretary Ricky Martin because she liked to sing in the shower, and because she suffered from the same blinding ambition as the actual Ricky Martin. Besides which, the real Ricky Martin was seven years old back then, or something. I think you get the point.

Ricky Martin was lovely, but she was hired by my mother, a woman not known for her intuition about people. Mom was famous for her attraction to the mentally ill (ex-husband number 1, shrink number 3, and so on and so forth). Ricky Martin was also an aspiring writer, which is never good. You see, dear reader, 90 percent of all writers (the exceptions are people in self-help groups, Mormons, Scientologists, and children of writers who are also writers) hate all other writers. And anyone who says differently is merely lying or is Steve Martin, who can love everyone because he's the best kind of writer, a *movie star*. Anyway, Ricky didn't like being Mom's ho. She wanted to go and write books about her humble background just off the six train on the Upper East Side. Nothing sparks creativity like hating your boss, especially if she's wildly successful at something you would love to be doing.

Around that time we had moved from poverty-stricken Westport, Connecticut, to a humble town house on Ninety-fourth Street, which was on the edge of a bad neighborhood back then, and pretty much every month the house would get broken into. Ricky Martin didn't much like being mugged, held at gunpoint, et cetera. Add into this equation the fact that she was pretty much hanging by a thread to her mental health, and bingo, we have a possible recipe for a memoir and a chance for a VIP room in McLean (or whatever the mental institution of the moment is).

Ricky Martin was not the only other person who was living with us during that wild, wild time in American history otherwise known as the eighties. Suzo, a Vietnamese immigrant, was also living with us, or at least hanging out pretty much every day, living off the fat of the land (fat which included change in between the couch cushions, leftover foie gras, the occasional half-empty bottle of Dom Pérignon left by the wine merchant who didn't pay taxes). Suzo had a mole on his cheek that was black and had black hair growing out of it. Suzo was otherwise a very nice-looking Vietnamese man in his late thirties or early forties or something. Margaret (my Upper East Side standard-issue nanny) liked Suzo; Suzo liked Margaret, though I wondered if he was just a tad brainwashed from all the Christian missionaries he had encountered in prewar Vietnam. Margaret and Suzo would have long conversations about Jesus, the church, the Lord's Prayer, and converting the infidels.

So in 1988, the town house on East Ninety-fourth Street existed as an earthly paradise, filled with saints, sinners, shoppers, sadists, socialites, socialists, and Mom's new secretary, who replaced the recently institutionalized Ricky Martin. Unfortunately the new secretary, whom we'll just call Winona Ryder (because of her erratic behavior and her love of all things from Saks), didn't last long. She had a brain tumor (here I am actually not being funny or at least not trying to be funny, the God's honest truth is that Winona Ryder did in fact have a brain tumor in her brain, and it was the size of a small golf ball by the time they took it out). This did not help her secretarial skills.

One day she was sitting at her desk in the front part of the basement of our house on Ninety-fourth Street (the sex doctors lived in the back part of our basement; please see "Sex Doctors" essay for more information on the Sex Doctors), answering the phone, trying to ignore the sounds of octogenarian pleasure coming from the room behind hers, and hanging out with our incontinent little white dog when Mom and I came downstairs to say hello. I was ten and going through my "I'm going to sue you" phase. I had heard that Mom and Dad had gotten litigious with each other a bunch of times. I had also been told that Mom had made the biggest mistake of her entire career and possibly her entire life when she had tried to sue Columbia Pictures. I understood that suing was something grown-ups did. It was that belief that inspired an interesting developmental phase marked by me telling everyone I came into contact with, "I'm going to sue you."

Winona was sitting at her desk. She was reading *TV Guide*.

"So," Mom said, "anybody call?" Mom had slightly ashy blond hair during the eighties. Tragically, Mom also wore patchwork clothing designed by Koos, a man talented enough to make even Nancy Reagan look like a soup kitchen frequenter.

"You know what I think, Erica?" Her eyes blazed with a

kind of passion found only in the pages of great magazines like *Us Weekly* and *InStyle*.

"Are there any messages for me? Maybe something from my agent," I said in my best Joan Collins.

"I have an idea," Winona said.

Mom and I stood on the staircase looking over at Winona's desk and her blank eyes.

"*Together,* we should buy an Epilady, and then we can share it."

"What's an Epilady?" I said.

"It's a thing that removes leg hair. It has three high-powered coils, and hair gets trapped in the coils, and it is removed at the root, get it, the root." Winona waved a brochure. "Erica and I can buy one together, and then we can share it. We can buy one at Saks."

"Ohh yeah, that's real normal," I said.

"Remember what I did the last time you spoke back to grown-ups?" Mom warned. Of course the problem with Mom's strict warning was that Mom's idea of punishment was pretty meek: no late-night TV watching for one night or no mad shopping trips for one day. What she had done the last time I had spoken back to a grown-up was ask me not to do it again.

Needless to say, the Epilady was just one of Winona's interesting ideas, which included her and Mom taking a weekend in Vegas to go gambling, and her and Mom getting matching tattoos. Mom and Winona never did get to share an Epilady; the incident was really the beginning of the end, and ultimately it left Mom again secretary-less. A few months later Winona was diagnosed with the brain tumor, it was taken right out, and she became totally normal again. Of course, by then Mom had found Mandy Moore.

Mom decided she'd never hire anyone who was actively hallucinating again, and so she hired Mandy Moore, who was not psychotic. Mandy was funny and happy like the real Mandy Moore. But unlike the real Mandy Moore, she did good secretarial work. And also unlike the real Mandy Moore, Mandy was a very butch lesbian from a very WASPy family. She spent much of her time on Fire Island building things: WASPy things like birdhouses and grouse huts. Mom enjoyed employing someone who didn't hallucinate or hear voices, but eventually Mandy decided to move to Fire Island and pursue grouse-hut building full-time, proving my thesis that all good people eventually quit their jobs to build grouse huts. Sadly, Mom's string of one good employee came to an abrupt end with Marie Osmond.

We'll call her Marie Osmond because of her incredible value system.

The first time I knew that Marie Osmond was probably stealing money from Mom was when she offered to write me a check out of Mom's bank account in return for some Valium (this was two years before I got clean, before I went to Minnesota and *maybe* joined an anonymous self-help group that helps millions of people every year). It was a hot day in August, and Mom was in Europe. Marie had short, dark hair. She was heavy. She hated Mom. She knew that she had at least one writer inside of her dying to get out. Marie was working on a novel about an oppressed, brown-haired secretary named Marie who had two daughters and a slightly scary husband—and hated her boss.

The first day it occurred to me that she was stealing from Mom, she was sitting at the desk in Mom's little studio office apartment, working on her novel while looking through the Neiman Marcus catalog.

I told Marie I didn't feel good about stealing from my mother. *Just kidding.* I told Marie to make the check out to cash! And so began my brief career as a forger and thief. I wish I could say I felt pangs of guilt for stealing from my own mother, but (and I think I illustrate an important point about employee theft when I say this) I felt there was so much money being spent on such stupid stuff that I felt it was my duty to steal it and put it to better use. You see, I knew I could save lives and make the world a better place with that money. I knew I could help a salesgirl at Barneys feel better about herself by helping a humble wallflower like myself turn into Zsa Zsa Gabor, Junior.

But secretaries and housemen are really just bare bones when it comes to the staff of the rich and famous. Every child needs at least one nanny, though two is always better and three nannies is like actually having a parent. Nannies' salaries start at five hundred dollars per week, but that's for the non-English-speaking, non-green-card-carrying, non-CPR-practicing ones with criminal records.

My first nanny was called Monica Lewinsky. She was a hulking Southern Baptist. Monica Lewinsky liked to cover me in Vaseline and tell Mom that she "greased that baby up." Now she'd be arrested for that, but back then (in the late seventies) they just took pictures. She took me to church, thus illustrating an interesting point about bohemians in general and my Jewish bohemian parents and grandparents in particular. Bohemians think they are open to everything, and they are, as long as it doesn't involve taking their infant daughter to a Baptist church to pray with stomping, shouting people who believe in Jesus.

My second nanny was called Kate Hudson. She was British. She ran off with the carpenter, who was also British. The carpenter never finished the roof.

My third nanny was called Marge Simpson. She was gay, and Mom thought that would prevent her from running off with the carpenter. It did; she ran off with Mom's yoga instructor. She was a trailblazer, leaving us for an activity that a mere two decades later the great cultural critic Christy Turlington would make famous.

My fourth nanny was called Sarah Jessica Parker (or Margaret), who is featured in almost every essay in this here book. She had had a husband named Bob, who was a truck driver. He'd died of Lou Gehrig's disease. Sarah Jessica Parker had four children. She taught me the Lord's Prayer. She also taught me about Moon Pies, polyester, and taking communion. Sarah Jessica Parker stayed with us for ten years; in fact she just stopped picking out my pink "tomorrow" outfit last year.

While nannies are expensive and often insane, they really aren't that much of an extravagance. Nannies are pretty much de rigueur on the Upper East and Upper West Sides. Even people in rural, poverty-stricken Westport, Connecticut, have nannies.

But not everyone has bodyguards. A good way to help

other people realize that you are in fact famous is to travel with a bunch of bodyguards. One might make you safe, but two or three will just make you safer and safer. Not to harp on Ricky Martin (now I'm talking about the real Ricky Martin), but Ricky reportedly travels with two assistants and at least one of each of the following: a personal chef, a driver, a makeup artist, a hairstylist, a yoga teacher, and a bodyguard.

I have always wanted a bodyguard. A bodyguard is proof that you aren't some lowly writer, some crack-smoking hack. A bodyguard is proof that you are a famous celebrity. Of course the only bodyguard I ever really got to know was Liza Minnelli's bodyguard Mohammed (and I am using the word *know* in only the most superficial way). He was a small man who looked as if he were made of stone. He had a very thick neck. I think he was Egyptian. He wasn't very talkative, but I didn't let that clue me in to the fact that he had no interest in discussing Liza's personal life with me. I once asked him (in the elevator) if he'd ever killed a man. He said nothing. This was what he usually said: nothing. I don't think he liked me. But luckily he didn't kill me. Liza (whom I only knew very, very vaguely and superficially from living in the same building) told me that Halston had left Mohammed to her in his will. The only thing I ever saw Mohammed do was walk Liza's little black dog, Lily. I never saw him kill a man, though I did see him on several occasions scoop the poop.

See, it all comes down to new math, which goes something like this: each bodyguard you employ makes you more famous, and thus in need of more security.

But enough about bodyguards. Bodyguards can only do so much; after all, they can't make you the most important thing . . . thin. In that respect the most important person to employ is a trainer (the trainer of the '00s is a yoga teacher; she's like the spiritual, pot-smoking trainer). Sure, Mom and I have worked out with trainers in the past: there was Andrey, the muscles from Hungary, who had horrible breath, spat when he talked, and ate only apples. Sure, Mom and I have worked out with yoga teachers: there was Jennifer, who hated her mother, dated only French men, and ate only organic foods. But working out with and employing full-time are two very different things. To be really famous one must employ a person full-time, because even in poverty-stricken Westport, Connecticut, people work out with trainers. To be really famous one must have one's own yogi, which brings me to an important question: Can one really be famous, I mean spiritual, without a spiritual adviser?

Nancy Reagan had a psychic; Sylvester Stallone's mom is a psychic; and Michael Jackson had a monkey named Bubbles. It's important when choosing a spiritual adviser to find one who's au courant. You don't want to be practicing Scientology if God is only listening to people who practice Kabbalah that month. A way to find out what religion works is to keep on top of what *InStyle* magazine says. God reads *InStyle* magazine monthly so he can decide who is faithful and who is an infidel.

I once observed a Kabbalah class at Showroom Seven (which is basically a store in the fashion district). I liked Kabbalah because Sandra Bernhard was there, and we all know that God likes famous people much, much better than he likes anyone else. I also liked the Kabbalah class because the Kabbalah rabbi was hot (in a very nebbishy way). I went to a few romantic kosher meals with the rabbi (I was young, he was not), and then I decided not to join the Kabbalah movement. The reason came down to the Zohar, the ancient Kabbalah text. The Zohar isn't translated, so one has to look (not *read* but look) at the twenty-seven volumes and scan the letters for energy. Now I've bought a lot of stupid shit in my life— violently expensive handbags, a Lots-a-Lots-a-Leggggggs, and a yogurt maker—but even I had to draw the line somewhere, and paying for religion is where I drew the line. It's one thing to buy a six-hundred-dollar cashmere sweater from Barneys but quite another to buy a six-hundred-dollar ten-encyclopedia set from God.

In the end I probably would have married the Kabbalah rabbi if I didn't feel so fucking cheap for not coughing up the dough for the Zohar. The rabbi did, however, continue to call me for months afterward, leading me to think one of two things: one, that I'm simply irresistible, and/or two, that it's not the easiest thing to date when you're a Kabbalah rabbi in New York City.

I never had a guru. I blame this on my mother. My childhood friend had a guru named Gurimi, who lived in South Fallsburg, New York. I often think that if I had had the benefit of a guru, my life might have turned out differently. I might today be a famous model like that friend, or at the very least I might have gone out with Mick Jagger. Either way, I never had a guru, and for that I am in therapy, which gets me to what I *did* have. I had a tutor. Rich kids in Manhattan who aren't the sharpest knives in the drawer are considered dyslexic: they are sent to tutors who do their homework and (best-case scenario) give them candy. I had many tutors to help me with my tragic, tragic illness, dyslexia, for which I suffered many minutes of tragic humiliation. But dyslexia has taught me so many important things, and in many ways dyslexia has saved my life: see, before dyslexia I was just some Jewish kid on the Upper East Side, but after dyslexia I was some Jewish kid on the Upper East Side with dyslexia.

My first tutor was called Mary Q. She was from New Zealand. She had yellow teeth. She was brought in on the case by the Dalton School right before they kicked me out. She was friends with my first shrink. Everybody has a first shrink, and mine was Doctor A, who was the worst shrink in the world and made me miss countless hours of television, which probably would have contributed more to my mental health in the long run.

Mary Q worked in an office on Seventy-fourth Street. She had piles of educational children's magazines in her office, along with the stray copy of *People* accidentally left in the corner by someone's well-meaning nanny. I think it's fair to say that Mary Q introduced me to *People* magazine, and for that I owe her a debt of gratitude I may never be able to repay. Yes, it's true, if I had had the benefit of a guru I might be a famous model today, but if I hadn't had a tutor I wouldn't be able to read the sentence "Calista Flockhart hasn't eaten solid food since 1996."

I know there were several tutors between Mary and Judy. I remember vaguely a fat woman in Norwalk who made me read off flash cards. But Judy R really stuck in my mind. I loved Judy because she gave me candy and I am a compulsive overeater. This is why I love candy and, furthermore, love everyone who gives it to me. Judy had a dark office on the tenth floor of a limestone prewar building on Ninety-sixth Street between Park and Madison Ave. Judy had a bowl of peanut M&M's in her office. Judy also had Oreos, candy corn, and chocolate chip cookies. Personally I have always loved candy corns. I have always loved the texture of them in my mouth. I have always loved the way they appear like magic around the time of Halloween and then disappear, only to be found at a rat-infested World of Nuts and Candy at a later date. I live for candy corns.

Judy was pretty and nice. I loved that she gave me candy. She was no guru, but she was an able-bodied candy pusher.

Speaking of pushers, if you want to be famous it is very important to have a drug dealer. A drug dealer is what separates the Christian Slaters and the Robert Downey, Jrs., of the world from the Scott Baios and the Ricky Schroeders. I think drug dealers should fall into the category of people on the payroll. My first drug dealer worked in Hell's Kitchen. Her name was Eleanor. She ran a comic book store that puzzlingly did not sell comic books. I'd call Eleanor a few hours before I wanted to come by, and then she would meet me with open arms and graciously accept my hundred dollars; in return, she would give me some fine marijuana. While Eleanor was no guru, nor was she a tutor, she did enjoy the virtues of stocking *People* magazine and nice, thick blunts of Jamaica's most lucrative export. Sadly, Eleanor went the way of many drug dealers (and many members of my family; just kidding; okay, I'm not), to jail with the other drug dealers. But the comic book store did not stay dark for long. Eleanor's son Albert soon took over the thriving business and made it thrive even more. Tragically, Albert liked to work out of his totally scary tenement in the West Nineties on Amsterdam, not far from my shrink. This was convenient for therapy, but sadly Albert too was soon arrested, along with his *Baywatch*-loving girlfriend and his ten pit bulls.

One of the great things about New York City is that when you lose one drug dealer you are able quite easily to find another. Sure, I'd probably never find another drug dealer who also had a comic book store, but that didn't matter to me. I knew that finding a good drug dealer had nothing to do with comic books and everything to do with convenience. And that's how I found Les, the automotive drug dealer. Les was truly more. I'd just phone up his convenient, law-abiding beeper and punch in my number. Then Les would call me back and arrange a place to meet. Usually Les drove a red Jeep and was black; sometimes, however, he drove a green Honda and had red hair. This hurt my relationship with Les: the fact that he was actually twenty different people working under the same name (also never knowing whether he was black or Hispanic or once Hasidic). But it also made me love Les. I bought drugs from Les throughout high school; he was pretty much my favorite educator. Sadly, Les couldn't do more than he could do; so I had to find someone who could deal more serious drugs.

That was when I met Felix. I always loved Felix. Like Les, Felix had the habit of being of different races and driving different cars. But Felix dealt much harder drugs. I bought drugs from Felix until I had to make the trip all fucked-up girls from the Upper East Side have to make: to rehab.

As you can see from this here essay, being Jennifer Lopez is incredibly challenging. Sometimes I think my life was hard, with the shopping and watching television and being paid attention to, but then I think of poor, poor Jennifer Lopez, who had to fly in private planes and have personal shrinks, trainers, doctors, closet organizers, food tasters, and cultural critics. In the final analysis I would say I paid and paid dearly for not having grown up with a guru: if I had, I might be one hundred feet tall in Times Square in my underwear extolling the virtues of Barelythere underwear. But if you get anything out of this essay, dear discouraged reader, it is that you too can be famous: all you need to do is hire a bodyguard, a chef, two nannies, a trainer, a guru, and a drug dealer.

the gentle gentile

*

THERE MAY HAVE BEEN sex doctors in my basement, but they weren't nearly as weird as the man I might have called Daddy. You see, it all started when I was seven years old. I was a spoiled brat. Luckily, so was my mother's boyfriend. He was only eighteen years older than I was. Consequently, we shared many similarities in taste and behavior. Both of us were cute, though only one of us looked like Annie. Both of us liked to watch *The Dukes of Hazzard, Diff'rent Strokes, The Facts of Life, Three's Company, A Different World,* and *The Cosby Show.* Both of us craved yellow marshmallow Peeps, green M&M's, vanilla Moon Pies, and caramel-flavored Tastykakes. We also both loved therapy, crying, and taking money from my mother.

For legal reasons, let's call Mom's boyfriend from the early eighties Dart. Dart is the name of the young, destructive lover in *Any Woman's Blues,* a novel by my mother, who wrote *Fear of Flying,* my mother, the feminist, who created the ideal sexual encounter, the zipless fuck. Sure, she wasn't quite Al Gore, who created the Internet, but the zipless fuck and her many other feminist ideas sold tons of books, and won her instant notoriety, the scorn of many of her peers, and the alarming title Queen of Erotica (you may remember a certain skinny journalist with nails like Barbra Streisand's who in the introduction to this here book was really harping on this whole Queen of Erotica thing).

It was summer. I was seven.

Dart grew up in a rotting Tudor mansion on the water in Darien, Connecticut. Dart's dad was wandering around looking for his glass of gin. He wore red velvet bedroom slippers and a quilted smoking jacket. All the medals (from sailing and tennis), all the certificates of achievement (from skiing and golf), all the newspaper clippings (of astonishing track times and unbelievable lacrosse scores), and other family victories (such as the time they sued their next-door neighbors for cutting down one of the family trees) were framed and displayed prominently in the guest bathroom.

Here are the things I remember about Dart's family's house: the smell of cat urine, the feel of cat litter between the floor and my shoe, and the stacks of yellow newspapers (*The New York Times, The Wall Street Journal,* the *New York Post,* the *Herald Tribune, Women's Wear Daily,* The *Darien Journal*) in precarious piles reaching almost to the crown moldings.

Dart's father showed my nanny Margaret and me how he shot the geese on his lawn with a real sawed-off shotgun. He explained to us that he had to shoot the geese because otherwise they would desecrate his lawn. Margaret didn't believe in killing things for drunken amusement, because she was and still is the best person who ever lived. Also, she is a saint. Margaret took me to mass every Sunday morning at St. Francis of Assisi Church. St. Francis was the patron saint of animals, including geese. Margaret liked geese.

That visit, Dart's mother made my mother a gin martini. Mom declined; it was eleven in the morning. A large cat named Mr. Bigglesworth scratched me. Dart's father went back outside to shoot more geese. Dart's mother started crying. Margaret gave me a vanilla Moon Pie. Mr. Bigglesworth pooped on the dirt around one of the potted plants. Dart's mother, face still slightly moist with tears, then tried to give me a musty needlepoint pillow that said, "Go first class or your heirs will."

Then Mom said it was time to go home. In the car ride home I asked Mom why Dart's mom was crying. Mom said, "In Darien it is the law that women must wear Belgian loafers, headbands, and loud pastel, floral Lilly Pulitzer dresses." She continued, explaining that "the headbands are tight and lead to early balding and to headaches."

Looking back on this, I am reminded of the Kitty Dukakis story, a made-for-TV movie where Kitty drinks rubbing alcohol to get a buzz on. Actually, now that I think about it, everything seems to remind me of the Kitty Dukakis story: my cousin's wedding, my first driving test, my first experience in a crack house, and my time in rehab. Kitty's story had nothing to do with Dart's family. Or maybe it did; maybe the story of the wife of the 1988 presidential candidate had everything to do with the Darts. There must have been a time when Michael Dukakis was more than a funny Greek guy with big eyebrows and no chance of winning the presidency.

Which leads me to the conclusion that there must have been a time when Dart's parents did more than wander around their moldy mansion musing about goose poop.

Dart lived over his parents' garage. It was a charming garage with water views, located in the best part of Darien. Every surface of Dart's garage apartment was covered in a thin layer of sticky beer film, coated with an even thinner layer of gray dust. The walls were covered with posters of half-naked women lying on cars, posters of half-naked women advertising various brands of beer, and posters of completely naked women lying on cars and advertising beer. A beanbag chair and many cardboard boxes created the illusion of furniture. AstroTurf graced the floor, conclusive proof that Dart would make a splendid fourth husband.

Dart proposed. He was twenty-four when he asked my mother to marry him. Mom said yes. This I did not like. I made Mom promise she wouldn't have any children with Dart. While I trusted her, I had to wonder if she was just telling me what I wanted to hear, aka lying. After all, we all knew that I could raise a serious ruckus when I wasn't getting what I wanted.

Then I thought about Dart. Dart said that all he wanted in life was a family. Why shouldn't he have wanted a family? His biological clock was ticking. He was twenty-four. His reproductive organs would only be working for what, another forty, maybe, fifty years. Evidence that Dart would be a good daddy was everywhere, from his Harley-Davidson motorcycle to his many tattoos. He even carried a switchblade and a gun.

It was the early eighties when Dart and Mom met. They

met in a class on Thucydides in the Harvard Ph.D. program in classics. No! They met in a mirrored weight room in a Gold's Gym in Darien.

Dart introduced himself as "an Aryan from Darien." She was amused. But he wasn't trying to be funny. Sure, he'd seen some Jews growing up—an estate lawyer, a bookkeeper, the friendly Jew who owned the local bagel shop, and a viola teacher named Murray. But he'd never known a Jew in the biblical sense (that he could remember; after all, he did go to Tulane University, which was chock-full o' Jews, and unfortunately also chock-full o' grain alcohol).

It seemed like the perfect match. He was twenty-four. She was thirty-nine. He needed a place to live. She needed to have the cabinets in the kitchen refinished. He was incredibly good looking. She was famous. He had a drug problem. She had a bichon frise named Emily Dogginson. He carried brass knuckles. She carried at least three shades of red Estée Lauder lipstick with her at all times. He smoked a lot of grass. She used Erno Laszlo black soap. He was in acting class with Lisa Bonet (which is almost like being on *The Cosby Show*). She'd been on *Carson*. He'd been incarcerated. A psychic once told her she was Cleopatra reincarnated. Both of them breathed, and both of them had cowboy boots. They were perfect for each other.

During the four years that Dart was my new daddy, he got into ten car and motorcycle accidents. Maybe their first date should have clued Mom in to the fact that he wasn't a very good driver. Dart came down to Weston, Connecticut, to let Mom make him tea. After tea, Mom asked Dart to leave because she wasn't the kind of girl who gives away the milk through the fence, thus preventing the ne'er-do-well from buying the cow. Dart was hesitant to leave because he thought that since she was Jewish she must control the banks and the media.

Mom made Dart leave.

It was snowing. Dart drove an old red Oldsmobile he had inherited from his one-legged uncle, Hiram. The driveway was steep and curvy. Uncle Hiram's Oldsmobile had seen two Kennedy assassinations. Its tires were balder than its original owner. Ravines surrounded Mom's narrow driveway. Uncle Hiram's Oldsmobile made one last groan as it skidded off the side of the steep driveway, careening down, down, down into the ravine.

Then Mom had to let Dart stay until the AAA people came. And somehow it took AAA a day and a half to come, and by the time they did, Mom and Dart were practically engaged.

The first few months were a blissful haze of leg warmers, big, baggy sweatshirt dresses, white Keds, rhinestones on inappropriate articles of clothing, and Tab. But then Lisa Bonet left Dart's acting class, and Dart suspected he wasn't going to get the part of Teito, Bill's illegitimate, white, WASP, alcoholic son, on *The Cosby Show,* and things started to head south.

Of course they didn't break up, they did what functional couples do: they stayed together for another four years. During those four years Dart tried to find himself, and Mom tried to find a way to get rid of him. Here are some of the methods she tried: lavishing expensive presents on him, yelling at him, dragging him to a certain gray muumuu-clad shrink for therapy (please see Shrinks essay for more details), stuffing him with health food, starving him with liquid diets, and making him have his crystals read. Finally she stumbled on the one thing that made Dart go home to his parents: AA.

But before being faced with AA, Dart encountered the sad reality of proximity to celebrity. Maybe Dart felt uncomfortable that people kept referring to him as "the child." Maybe Dart minded that he spent most of his time with Mom waiting for television interviews, in green rooms that were almost never green. Maybe Dart didn't like the nagging feeling that he was nothing on his own, the crushing self-doubt, the way all his accomplishments looked pathetic up against Mom's. I liked (and still do) sitting in green rooms (mostly because I love muffins), and all my accomplishments also looked pathetic next to my mom's. Of course at the time I was seven. This was about the time I started calling Dart "The Vagabond" 'cause I saw Joan Collins do it in *Dynasty*.

I think Dart could have freed himself from the sticky wicket of what to do with his life by doing what most literary spouses and offspring do (and I do often and always): Dart should have written a thinly veiled autobiographical novel (please see first novel, *Normal Girl*). Eventually Dart did write a memoir, though it was never published. Unfortunately Dart had only the vaguest notion of how the English language works; due to his education at a very WASPy boarding school that catered to the more dim-witted children of the wealthy, he was versed in lacrosse rather than in Lord Byron, and in tennis rather than in Tennyson.

Other people might have suggested that Dart get a job. Dart had only a select range of skills. He could have been a drug dealer or a politician. But Dart was really too honest to be a politician.

Dart knew people thought he should get a job. Responding to this tremendous social pressure, Dart thought a lot about working. He even talked a lot about working, and maybe all those hours he was sleeping he dreamed a lot about working. He slept a lot. Margaret said it was because he was a slob and because he was taking *tons* of drugs.

Margaret hated Dart. She said Dart was a bum (that did seem to be the consensus). She said Dart was a cheat and a drug addict. Personally, I think she hated Dart because he was a Protestant.

As for his alleged career, Dart had a conflicted relationship with acting. He acted with zeal when Mom found out he was having an affair. He acted a lot about the girl at the A & P supermarket. He acted as if he didn't know her. He acted as if he wasn't the father of her child. He acted as if he hadn't taken those nudie pictures of her. But Dart never did the kind of acting you get paid for. I guess you could say he didn't want to prostitute his art.

So the eighties continued: *Spy* magazine thrived, the movie *Dirty Dancing* won our hearts and minds, Princess Fergie got married, and Mom and Dart stayed together. Margaret bought me a pink velour sweat suit with arms that zipped off. Mom got me the pony. Dart pretty much carried on at his usual speed.

Then, shocking the many therapists whom they'd seen, surprising the women who worked in the A & P, and stunning my Jewish middle-class family, Dart and Mom split. In

spite of Dart's desire to be a daddy, in spite of his possible im-
pregnation of the woman who worked at the A & P, in spite
of Mom and Dart's meeting in a gym, in spite of his drug
problem and her successful career, the relationship tragically
burned out after four or five short years.

And so on a cold day in June, on a walk around the reser-
voir in Weston, Connecticut, little, blond Mom told tall,
lanky, brown-haired mustached Dart:

"You have to stop doing drugs and you have to go to AA
if you want to stay with me."

To which he replied: "But baby, I love you and I love our
life together, especially my motorcycle. Ain't my motorcycle
cool, baby?" (Okay, he might not have said that, but he un-
doubtedly said something equally clueless.)

Mom stood uncharacteristically firm. But even with the
help of AA, Dart couldn't stop doing drugs, even if he had
wanted to. So Dart moved back to his lovely apartment over
his parents' garage in scenic Darien. Mom made Dart's study
into a conversation pit with levels carpeted in the latest
brown carpeting. I was happy to see Dart go, really happy.
I didn't have anyone around to practice my moves from *Dynasty* on, but I got complete attention from my mother and
from Margaret. I also got extra "play" sessions with Doctor A,
although Docter A's favorite game was the absurdly sucky
Talking, Doing, and Feeling (a therapeutic board game). For
a brief second, Mom was single, Margaret was dragging us all
to an absurd amount of church, and all was quiet.

Then Mom got married to the one man you can never
divorce, a divorce lawyer. Thank God, they lived happily ever
after and years went by. *Dynasty* went off the air, rhinestones

went out, Madonna stopped wearing underwear outside of her clothing, and Keds were replaced with Doc Martens.

We went to live in a hideous white brick building in the East Sixties, with the lovely Jewish divorce lawyer, whose parents owned a very reputable linen supply business. For a while it was odd for Mom and me to have a man in our lives who went to work, who didn't drive a motorcycle, who didn't disappear for days on end, and who didn't sling the crack rock. Somehow we adjusted.

With the addition of a standard poodle and some Ben Shahn drawings, Mom and the divorce lawyer were able to live the bohemian bourgeois fantasy.

Life went along, a new century dawned: Madonna became British, *Mademoiselle* went out of business, the Cold War ended, Prozac became standard issue, and Yoga became the chic exercise of choice.

Then one day in the month of either January or July or possibly March, Dart came to Mom's wooden house in Weston. I was at that very moment in a Best Western in Troy, Michigan, with an earnest young editor, visiting his adoring mother, who smoked two packs of cigarettes a day and owned an overweight dog. I was in my early twenties. I had sampled the huge block of headcheese that is life. I had dropped out of a few colleges, graduated from an illustrious rehab, attended a smattering of self-help meetings, been to Atlantic City four times, done jury duty, slept with a man in the armed services, and watched more television than some people watch in a lifetime.

Though I had changed and grown thinner, my change was nothing in the face of Dart's transformation from chiseled twenty-four-year-old stud on a motorcycle to beer-bellied old guy with a crumb-filled mustache, two children, and an ulcer he called Larry.

Dart was back. He did not come to stalk Mom, he did not come to ask her to blurb his memoir, he did not come because he missed her.

It was a cloudy day in April, May, or November, and he was driving a truck. Not the kind of truck one usually sees in the swank suburban suburb of Weston, Connecticut. Dart was not driving a BMW SUV. He was not driving a Range Rover. He was not even driving a Hummer. This truck did not have fuel injection. This truck did not have a fin or cruise control. It did not have leather seats or seat warmers. It did not have GPS. It did not even have a CD player. Dart's ride was not for leisure. It was for work. Dart had parlayed his love of acting into a lucrative career selling meat from a truck.

How does one get into the meat-selling business? I don't know how you get into that business or any other, because I've never had a job. Well, that's not true, I once worked for a gallery, but Mom had to pay them, so I don't know if that counts as a job. Back to Upton Sinclair's favorite topic. Did I mention that this meat is vacuum-packed for freshness and quality? Did I tell you that this meat is "restaurant-style" meat?

On the day that Dart came down the driveway (past the place where he'd slid off a decade before) to Mom's house, the ex-lovers reunited, unbeknownst to my stepfather or to me. This time Mom's attraction took the form of commerce. Mom bought a side of beef, forty lamb chops, one hundred chicken wings, twenty-five beef fillets, seventeen swordfish steaks, twenty-six salmon steaks, fifteen fillets of Dover sole, twelve bison steaks, and twenty-seven crab cakes. Dart arranged all the frozen meat in her freezer and then presented her lovingly with a bill for seven hundred dollars.

After months and months of pork-sicles, the divorce lawyer and I started to get suspicious. We were slightly confused as to where all the frozen meat had come from. We didn't know about Dart's little visits. We didn't know about Dart's big career shift. First Mom told us the frozen meat fairy had brought it. But I wasn't fooled, and the divorce lawyer had wised up since Mom had tried to pawn off the appearance of a bunch of handbags on the Prada fairy.

I looked at Ken. He was frying up some crab cakes. We stood in the kitchen of my mom's Weston house. The whole house smelled really bad because Mom and Ken burned glossy color magazines, releasing toxic fumes into my delicate little lungs. I could hear *People* magazine sizzling in the fireplace.

Ken and I proceeded to confuse her.

"Mom," I asked, looking deep into her blue eyes, "Mom, who is selling you meat?"

"No one," she said, smiling. Mom always smiled when she lied.

"No one at all?" I asked.

"No."

"Are you sure, Mom?"

"No." Mom was grinning up a storm now.

"Yes?"

"No," she said.

"So no one?"

"No," she said.

"So that's a no?"

"Yes? No, Dart wasn't selling me frozen meat. I mean, I mean no one was selling me frozen meat." Ken and I fell into fits of hysterical laughter. My copy of Cosmo sizzled in the fire. Yet another Jong mystery was solved; Mom was buying meat from Dart's meatmobile.

More had to be done, though. For you see, dear reader, our freezer was bursting with bison. We'd had enough of pork chop–sicles. Mom went out to the meatmobile, all five feet, three inches of her, in adorable pink sneakers. She told Dart he needed to go sell meat to someone else. I had thoughtfully compiled a list of book reviewers in the local area who might be interested in buying some frozen vacuum-packed meats.

After being told he couldn't sell us meat anymore, Dart disappeared. He flew off like a meat-selling angel. His wings were made of baby lamb chops; his tail made of frozen lobster tail; his ample angel bosom made of crab cakes; and his hair white like tartar sauce. I guess it was just Dart's time to stop getting money from my mother. I hope that time never comes for me.

Ultimately my life was changed by Dart. Yes, Dart darted into my life like a young, talentless playboy, but he taught me cheesy lessons that not even good old Morrie could have taught me on Tuesdays. Yes, Dart taught me valuable life lessons: selling meat from a truck is more lucrative than acting. Ex-girlfriends will buy meat from a truck if it's vacuum-packed. It's better to marry a burly Jewish divorce lawyer than a twenty-four-year-old disenfranchised WASP with a motor-cycle. The Jews do not control the banks and the media (at least not all the banks). Bison is a tasty snack. Sometimes slinging crack rock is not a sign of a larger substance abuse problem. Driving is difficult. And a friendship with Lisa Bonet won't get you into most co-ops.

the sex doctors in the basement

*

THIS IS A STORY about sex, about drugs, about the sex doctors who lived in our basement, about a rotting town house on Ninety-fourth Street, and about two French Freudian analysts who, like all French people, enjoyed the comedy of Jerry Lewis. *Please note that these analysts were not the sex doctors, they were merely the previous tenants. Coincidence? I think not.*

You see, once upon a time two French Freudian analysts (who were weird but not the sex doctors) lived on Ninety-fourth Street in a narrow town house that was painted various shades of dark olive. They saw their patients in their basement, which was soundproofed. They often ate baguettes and olives. They liked to drink French wine and French fizzy water, because they were French, or something, who knows. Then they moved out; the quiet, Proust-loving, Freud-worshiping, Jerry Lewis–quoting French analysts moved out in 1982, and in came every co-op board's worst nightmare, the Jongs.

Let me start at the beginning, way before the era of the Kronhausens (the actual sex doctors who lived in our basement—not to be confused with the French analysts who were the previous tenants) and their best friends, the free radicals (free radicals are broken atomic bonds that may or may not cause premature aging). Did I mention that my parents were married briefly in the eighties? Well, they were. They were married for thirty long months, from approximately the premiere of *Dallas* on television to the election of Ron Reagan. I would like to interject a little interjection here and say *Thank God* Mom and Dad got divorced. I have never known of two people more wrong for each other than my mom and my dad. Anyway, Mom bought the town house on East Ninety-fourth Street for two reasons. One thing was my almost stepfather Dart. Not many co-op boards looked kindly on my twenty-four-year-old almost step-pa. And his collections of flasks and ammo did not help the situation. Though surely if the co-op boards had heard about him being in the same acting class as the great Lisa Bonet they would have taken a liking to him faster than you can say "Maidstone [a very restricted club in the Ho-ho-Hamptons] is not a restricted club." The other reason Mom decided on the East Ninety-fourth Street town house was because Mom wanted a place where she could for the first time make a home that was hers. And hers it was.

In the early eighties, the city was teeming with pickpockets, squeegee men, muggers, and people who had recently been released from mental institutions (thank you, Ronald Reagan, or should I say "Gipper"?). The city wasn't safe: people like Robert Chambers drank at Dorian's, people like Zandra Rhodes were making us wear clothing kept together with safety pins, and somewhere at any given moment *WKRP in Cincinnati* was being aired. Ninety-fourth Street sat right next to Ninety-fifth Street, which in turn sat next to Ninety-sixth Street, which was the beginning of Spanish Harlem. Ninety-sixth Street was the barrier. On one side of Ninety-sixth Street there were million-dollar town houses; on the other side, tenements. On one side of Ninety-sixth Street kids went to private schools in town cars accompanied by nannies. On the other side of Ninety-sixth Street kids fought for desks at understaffed public schools. On one side of Ninety-sixth Street there were health insurance and fancy specialists. On the other side of Ninety-sixth Street children still died of preventable childhood diseases. It was like living in Berlin except that, instead of communism being to blame for this discrepancy in wealth, it was capitalism.

I remember the first time I ever saw the East Ninety-fourth Street town house. It was a cold day in November when Mom brought Dart, my nanny Margaret, and me to look at the house. I remember the sounds of cooing pigeons (trying to get rid of these pigeons would bring Mom to the brink of madness), and the homeless wino we stepped over to begin our ascent up the crumbling brownstone steps. Margaret grabbed the wobbly metal handrail; a large chunk of black paint fell off in her hand. I remember looking up at the handrail, at the other brownstones on Ninety-fourth Street, all of them leaning precariously on one another, at the chipped limestone pavement and wondering (even at the age of seven) whether this thing was structurally sound or not. Please note the next sentence; the one directly after this one is meant to be sarcastic; taking this sentence any other way will lead to immediate and permanent dislike of our protagonist (me), which you may come to anyway but which should not not not result from this next sentence, which is actually meant to satirize a sentence from a typical memoir, although of course this sentence is also a commentary on mediocre satire, or a commentary on memoir, or a commentary on run-on sentences, or possibly, as my hero Woody Allen says, "*Commentary* and *Dissent* have merged, forming a new journal called *Dysentery*." Of course I was very sophisticated for my age—I had already been cooed at by such luminaries as Dr. Ruth Westheimer and Loretta Swit (what ever happened to her?).

And so Mom bought the East Ninety-fourth Street house from two French analysts who loved the color dark olive. Mom liberated herself from the oppression of being a successful novelist by painting her town house pink and hanging paintings of naked lesbians having sex (sorry, Mom, but Sabrina G and I are still traumatized from seeing the painting that hung above the stairs).

Now, contrary to that report on Page Six, not every room in the town house was hot pink. The walls in my room were covered with little purple flowers. Mr. Pig (please see "My New Daddy Is a Jailbird" for further explanation) said it looked like a bordello. He was, of course, wrong; our house didn't look like a bordello. Our house looked like every other house on the Upper East Side that had a hot pink door and purple rooms, pink rooms, and paintings of ladies playing naked Twister. Yes, life seemed quite normal back then in the early eighties, in New York, in our town house with the pink door, until one day a certain actress went *Out on a Limb* after taking *A Journey of the Spirit*. Yes, she *Didn't Fall off the Moun-*

tain, thank *My Lucky Stars* for that. Instead she found *You Can Get There from Here,* and so she went back *Out on a Limb, Going Within,* and found she could *Dance While She Could* and kicked the sex doctors out of her sprawling Central Park West apartment once and for all.

Life might have been normal before, but once Shirley MacLaine got rid of her houseguests, whom she had hosted for over five years, life took a turn for the very, very weird. When they came into our lives, Phyllis and Eberhard Kronhausen were trying to find the cure for death, or at least trying to knock that pesky Dr. Atkins off the *New York Times* bestseller list. How they got into health wasn't immediately clear. Eberhard was originally from Berlin and he was in his seventies. He smelled like the fish oil pills he took every day to keep from dying. He looked like he was a hundred years old. His wife, Phyllis, was from the Midwest. She was only in her mid-fifties, but she also looked as if she was a hundred and three. Both of them were Dachau thin, yellow from tanning and fish oil, and really, really wrinkly. Both of them liked to wear luminous polyester tracksuits, to drink carrot juice and ramble about the wonders of beta-carotene while swinging their arms violently as they power-walked though Manhattan's Central Park.

The path to trying to cure death had started in the late 1940s, when the Kronhausens had gotten their Ph.D.'s in psychology. Soon after, they developed a theory similar to that of Dr. R. D. Laing, who believed that schizophrenics were just normal people who needed a little bit of love to realize they were not Moses.

And so the Kronhausens, guided only by their misguided

notions and a desire to follow the zeitgeist wherever it might go, decided to go live with some schizophrenics in a treatment center. Needless to say, the Kronhausens were wrong. Even with lots of love, the schizophrenics still believed they were Moses. Sadly, this did not discourage the Kronhausens, who clearly had never been exposed to the Fast-Mirsky manifesto, which states that at the first signs of failure, one should give up.

The zeitgeist then took them to Paris. In 1960s Paris, Phyllis and Eberhard became filmmakers. They were the Merchant-Ivory of their time; that is, if Merchant-Ivory made movies about naked circus performers. The Kronhausens were responsible for such titles as *The Hottest Show in Town* (also called *La Foire aux Sexes: Circus Kronhausen*), *Freedom to Love,* and *Danish X Cinema.* Yes, Phyllis and Eberhard showed that "pretty boy" Ismail (Merchant, the producer of *The Golden Bowl* and *A Room with a View*) how to really party.

Yes, Phyllis and Eberhard shared bodily fluids with most of the Boulevard Raspail in Paris, ah oui! They were also responsible for starting the Museum of Erotic Art. Basically Paris owes the Kronhausens a debt of gratitude for accelerating the spread of herpes in the Sixth Arrondissement (just kidding, there were no STDs back in the sixties, only white patent leather boots, bouffant hairstyles, the music of Elvis Presley, and the preaching and teaching of the Reverend Sun Myung Moon).

Why were so many famous and unfamous people attracted to the Kronhausens? They weren't good looking. They had stringy necks and weird accents. They weren't rich. But they had something about them that made people want to share bodily fluids with them. It was their quest to cure death that made people love them. No one wants to be on the forefront of antiaging more than celebrities, and that's why they flocked to the Kronhausens, and even why they shared bodily fluids with them.

But let's move beyond bodily fluids, shall we? After all, this isn't the Kronhausens' story, this is my memoir, God damn it. Of course it's only my first memoir. I have at least three more to go just about grade school. Watch out, Elizabeth Wurtzel; I suffered, too. For example, sometimes when the girl in the coffee place on the corner runs out of doughnuts, I have to get in a taxi and go all the way down to Eighty-third Street to get Krispy Kreme doughnuts. When that happens I am reminded of all the other hardships I have faced in my life, like not being able to get the forty-legged Lots-a-Lots-a-Legggggggs because my dad forgot to put his name on the wait list (see, Dad, the memory still haunts me to this day).

In the seventies the Kronhausens went to India, where they met Shirley MacLaine and also got diarrhea from the water. Then in the eighties the Kronhausens got into free radicals, which they thought were radical, and shortly after that they enter into our lives—more specifically, into our soundproof basement. No one had really been down to the basement since Mom had bought the place and the French analysts had left. Sure, Dart kept some guns down there, who didn't? And it's possible that Dart was also keeping pages of his memoir down there (hey, Mom's not the only one who can write, she's just the only one who can earn money from her writing).

Okay, I'm lying, I do remember going down to the basement once. I went with Margaret and food, of course. It was Easter time and marshmallow Peeps had surfaced. I love yellow Peeps. I also love blue Peeps. I love the grainy sugar on the outsides. But I didn't really get into Peeps until I was a bit older (last year); back then I was really just into Cadbury's cream eggs, the ones that are filled with sugar cream that looks like yolk.

In the basement, I just remember seeing all these old X-rays and file cabinets and files. Seems as if the analysts left tons and tons of their old patient files. Margaret always said she liked to read so much that if there were nothing else to read on earth, she'd read the labels on soup cans. Luckily, she didn't need to read soup cans. I didn't really understand the case files due to the sad fact that I was ten years old, and also because I was seriously dyslexic.

Margaret understood the case files because she'd seen the Granada Television version of *Brideshead Revisited*. Margaret understood everything—she read *Reader's Digest*. (Did I mention I'm seriously considering becoming a dentist?)

The basement was gross. It had dirty white, nubby wall-to-wall carpeting dating from the time the Kronhausens were into schizophrenics. It had double doors between all the soundproof rooms. The walls were all brown. The windows looked out on our garden, which was a doggy poop museum with poop dating to the late seventies, when Uri Geller was big. If I could be any celebrity, I'd totally be Uri Geller in a minute. They just don't bend spoons the way they used to.

But the scariest thing about the basement (besides the fact that the street entrance to it was under the stairs through a dark hallway, besides the reality that the basement was getting broken into about once a month) was what was below, the real basement, the seventh circle of Dante's Inferno. Because, you see, our basement was really just the garden apartment, and below the garden apartment lurked the real basement. I went down there once to that black, black hole of despair where two hundred years of other people's trash lived harmoniously with bugs, rats, and the most important element in any home lived in by people with irritable bowel syndrome, the septic tank.

On my journey down there it had been spring up in the garden apartment. Margaret had been my guide through that dark, dark world. Before we had gone, we took sustenance, feasting on the nectar of the gods (Coca-Cola) and Twinkies. We went down there on a mission, with a man who I will call Ross Perot even though he wasn't Ross Perot, he was the plumber, and we were on a mission to find the septic tank. Margaret knew a lot about plumbing because she has seen all ten hours and fifty minutes of the BBC production of *I, Claudius*. And I knew a lot about plumbing because I'd been on the *QE2* once. (Okay, neither of us knew anything about plumbing, or anything else, for that matter.)

One of the last things I remember from that challenging childhood hardship was walking down the rickety stairs with only a flashlight, two adults, and a box of Twinkies. I remember hearing the whistling of the pipes. I remember becoming enveloped in Dickensian darkness.

I can't tell you what I saw down there. I wish I could, but some childhood memories are too painful to bring back (like the Lots-a-Lots-a-Legggggggs, Dad). Yes, some things are too tragic to remember. And some things are just too boring to remember. The basement would fit nicely into that second category. But enough about me, let's get back to bodily fluids, shall we?

At this point the zeitgeist had taken the Kronhausens to Harper & Row, who had recently bought the idea for *Formula for Life*, which was a whole new Kronhausen. *Formula for Life* was a real solid departure from *Sex Histories of American College Men, The Sexually Responsive Woman, The Sex People: Erotic Performers and Their Bold New Worlds, Erotic Art,* and of course no Kronhausen bibliography would be complete without the great oeuvre *Erotic Art 2*.

My Catholic nanny Margaret (who prayed every morning and night, mostly for our souls) liked Phyllis and Eberhard because they were doctors (and because nobody told her about the circus of seminal fluids). I loved Margaret and always will (and not just because she introduced me to the Moon Pie, either.) Sometimes I might make fun of her for her God-loving ways, but the truth is that Margaret was just the greatest, nicest, kindest, sanest, most loving person in the entire world (and she had this really cool tricycle with huge wheels that we rode through the trailer park in Florida that she lived in.) Just because she didn't sleep with Anaïs Nin in Paris, or because she didn't appear in any Andy Warhol movies, didn't mean she wasn't a good nanny.

But I haven't really explained to you what Phyllis and Eberhard were like. Phyllis and Eberhard were more than just bad smells and thick accents. Phyllis and Eberhard were guests, professional guests. They sang for their supper. They told us stories about Paris with Henry, India with Shirley, and their work with the free radicals. Eberhard and Phyllis sort of tried to act like the bohemian grandparents I never had; the only problem was that I already had bohemian grandparents who painted in the Catskills, played drums in Harlem, read books like *Beyond Viagra*, drank from a flask, and smoked tea. My grandparents may not have done it with Anaïs Nin, but they were my actual grandparents.

Besides impersonating my grandparents, the Kronhausens also did small chores like dog walking and gardening, two things that otherwise just would never have gotten done (Mom was too busy fighting the pigeon problem at that point, and fight them she did, with everything from poison to small metal prods).

Anyway, it was 1983, and the United States had just invaded Grenada, which I think is near Vancouver. Mom and I were living at East Ninety-fourth Street with Dart (who had just turned twenty-five and was now old enough to legally buy spray paint), Phyllis and Eberhard Kronhausen, who had just begun their three-year tenure with the Jongs, and Margaret. Mom vogued for such great cultural journals as *New York Woman, Mirabella, Spy, New Woman, Lear's,* and *Buzz.* I was also a forerunner, just in a different way; my pink rhinestone sweat suits were taking the elite Manhattan private school Dalton by storm.

Of course I was about two years away from being asked to leave the high-powered prep school for inferior academic performance. I guess I just wasn't up to the academic standards of such intellectual luminaries as Chevy Chase, star of *Caddyshack I* and *II*; Tony Hiss, son of Alger; and Claire Danes, star of *The Mod Squad.* Manhattan private schools have standards they must keep up, since they have produced some of the great thinkers of our time.

It was 1983, the year of the Cabbage Patch Kid, the year of *Return of the Jedi,* and the year of the introduction of another great American fiction, the Star Wars missile defense program (thank you, Gipper). Life was peaceful and placid; the Kronhausens took little Poochini (our hopelessly stupid white fluffy bichon) for walks in Central Park. Poland lifted the state of martial law that had been in effect for the last nineteen months. Mom was about to publish a book that would really annoy Dad called *Parachutes & Kisses.* Dad was about to really annoy Mom by having another child, handsome, darling Ben, who is both single and a freshman at Princeton (again, bfast@princeton.edu). Though none of this annoyance would last for long, because a mere twenty years later my parents would bury the hatchet (during those twenty years the Cold War ended, apartheid ended, a sheep was cloned, the Berlin Wall fell, Britney Spears was hatched and grown, and the Balkans became separate countries).

Life was wonderful with our houseguests, the unflappable Kronhausens. Mom worked, Margaret nannied, Dart discovered a magical substance called cocaine, and I ate. The Kronhausens continued their tenure as basement residents. They slept on a white foldout couch that had been left by the French analysts. The Kronhausens worked on *Formula for Life.* They took lots of vitamins. They fought the free radicals, and all the while they looked like very tan human shar-peis. Sharpeis who I hope didn't exchange any bodily fluids with anyone, not even each other.

Sometimes the Kronhausens would take me with them

for Nazi death walks in Central Park (because I was fat and everyone was constantly trying to make me less fat). I didn't really understand who they were, I just thought they were funny old people like Helmut Newton and Dr. Ruth, except these old people lived in our basement. The Kronhausens were pretty boring; mostly they would swing their arms and talk about different kinds of fruits, vegetables, and sexual positions they tried with Anaïs Nin (just kidding, the Kronhausens were always very appropriate with me, unlike many members of my actual family). Then they would power-walk me home, and usually around that time Dart would come downstairs with a runny nose and a bad case of the munchies.

I often wonder what I was feeling back then. I often try to connect with the little fat girl who lived on Ninety-fourth Street. But even when I was her, I still didn't know too much about her. I don't remember ever feeling much, honestly. Do kids even have feelings?

So the eighties continued. A musical about mentally retarded people dressed up as cats (called *Cats*) was a smash hit, proving again the nonexistence of God. Rock Hudson died of AIDS. Sometime in August of 1985 Ronald Reagan may or may not have secretly sent arms to Iran. Who knows? Chernobyl happened. The *Challenger* exploded. Spuds MacKenzie hocked beer. Gary Hart got caught committing some monkey business. The market crashed, but more distressing than that was the popularity of little white canvas sneakers called Keds.

Soon it was winter again, we were heading toward the end the eighties, and Mom was feeling less in love with her lazy, drug-addicted, money-hemorrhaging soul mate. Mom was also feeling a little less in love with her houseguests.

Luckily, Mom was still in love with her little girl. You see, no matter what, my mom always loved me more than she loved anyone else.

Eberhard and Phyllis knew how to spot a trend, and while they were still working on their great masterpiece *Formula for Life,* they sensed it was time to move on. Let's face it, the stock market crash was about to herald a new era. Mom was getting sick of having twenty parasites living off her at all times, Mom was tiring of supporting her young, drug-addicted, motorcycle-riding boyfriend, Mom wanted to trim the fat. And trim the fat she eventually did; today she only has one bloodsucking money-extracting parasite in her life (I love you, Mommy).

Eberhard and Phyllis could read the writing on the wall. They'd been here before when the schizophrenics were like, "Leave me alone, okay, I'm Jesus." And when that certain actress (who's the sister of the man who starred in the worst movie ever, yes, that's right, the appalling remake of *An Affair to Remember*) tired of their smelly, vitamin-peddling charms. Yes, sometimes it's time to follow the zeitgeist to someone else's home. And so a mere three years later the Kronhausens moved out. They went to Costa Rica to a farm they had bought with the advance from *Formula for Life.*

Soon Dart took his guns, ammo, knives, motorcycle, and funny white powder to a place where these things seemed more normal, his parents' house in Darien.

The world was changing. We could all sense it in the air. We knew it. The world was about to become an entirely different place. Yes, Mom was only about four years from meeting a man who would change our lives forever with free legal work and a keen eye for documents. Mom was only about four years away from meeting husband number 4, a man the eminent cultural arbiter Joan Collins once called "dishy." And we could already feel it coming, the change.

I saw the sex doctors once more, after my childhood was long over and I was in fact pregnant with my first child. I saw them at a party my mother had for a book about anti-Semitism. It was July in New York City, and we were all sweating. I looked bloated and fat even though I was only three months pregnant. They looked amazing in their wrinkly way. Mostly they looked exactly the same. Almost two decades had passed, and they looked exactly the same.

"So, Molly." Eberhard was drinking white wine as he grabbed my arm. "What are you up to these days?"

I was able to push his wrinkly old hand off my arm. His teeth were yellow. He smelled like fish oil.

"Yes, Molly, what are you doing with your life?" said Phyllis.

I don't know why, but at that moment they were the scariest people I'd ever seen, between the enormous yellow teeth and the sagging skin—I wanted nothing more than to get far, far away from them.

"Go get her a copy of *Formula for Life*," Eberhard barked at Phyllis, white wine swishing around in his glass.

"Ohh, yes, I will get her a copy of *Formula for Life*."

Phyllis came back with a copy of *Formula for Life*. I glanced at it. "You must read it," Eberhard said. "This *Formula for Life* will change your life."

It was at that second that I remembered their nickname: America's guests. They were trying to wrangle some room at chez Jong-Fast. A year of them living in my living room flashed before my eyes. "There's no room for you to stay with us. Sure, of course we'd love it. But we only live in a one-bedroom apartment. I have to go."

"Read the book, you must read the book."

"Sure, whatever. We live in a one-bedroom apartment, no room, no room at the inn." Then I was able to slip back into the crowd of Jews, all of whom were thinking of one thing and one thing only. Okay, maybe two things: one—anti-Semitism, and two—how to muscle in and get to the lox.

Even though the sight of them disgusted me, I will still always remember my time with Phyllis and Eberhard. Even though the idea of the sounds of them making sweet love horrified me. Even though they never freed the radicals. Even in spite of all these things, I still love their wrinkly turkey necks. I only wish they were here living on my sofa, so I could give them a big ol' hug.

how an obese, muumuu-wearing

fascist helped me lose weight

*

I THINK IT'S IMPORTANT to mention something that I have observed. The more famous the parent, the more shrinks for the child of said famous parent. I think this is because famous people are obsessed with their children's mental health.

My mom was no Phyllis Diller, and so I had only four serious shrinks growing up. My first shrink was Doctor A. Doctor A would look deeply into my eyes and say:

"Tell me about your relationship with your mother."

I was eight. "I think you're a dork, Doctor A."

"Do you think having a mom who writes erotica is affecting your sense of well-being?"

I picked up the digital clock that Doctor A was intermittently staring at. "This time isn't right, Doctor A. I think this clock is about thirty-five minutes too slow." I started trying to change the numbers.

Doctor A was in her mid-forties. She had a nervous condition which manifested itself in her habit of constantly pushing her brown hair out of her eyes. Doctor A weighed slightly more than a hundred pounds. Almost all female shrinks in Manhattan are super skinny because otherwise no one would ever listen to them (due to the New Yorker's innate hatred of anyone weighing more then Paris Hilton's Chihuahua). "The clock is not wrong. Now tell me about your mother." She looked at me earnestly.

I looked back at her earnestly. "Can I get some candy? I love candy. Well, actually, now that I think about it . . ."

"What? Now that you think about it."

"I truly love the Tastykake Crumpet."

"Please, Molly, focus."

"I love the caramel."

"Molly, where are you?"

"Doctor A, I think you're a dork."

"That's not a very nice thing to say. Tell me about your mother."

That exchange pretty much sums up four years of therapy. I hated Doctor A because she was annoyingly earnest, because she gesticulated like a crack-addicted toy poodle, and mostly because she didn't give me candy.

Doctor R gave me candy and was a social worker with a long Greek name and an apartment on Central Park West. I thought she was dumb. Sometimes she would listen to her answering machine and open her mail during our sessions;

those were the times I liked her best. Sometimes she would stare at me and ask things like, "Do you feel repressed because your mother writes dirty books?" I was eleven.

Doctor L did not give me candy but did seem to have some clue as to what he was doing, which makes him totally stand apart from Doctor R and Doctor A. Doctor L had a fancy office between Madison and Fifth Avenue. Doctor L looked like an owl, and this was wildly amusing to me because his initials spelled owl, too. Once he gave me a piece of cake. I also liked him because his professional-looking office (old leather couches and expensive dried flower arrangements) actually was an office and was not in his living room. Doctor L wouldn't let me play with the dollhouse in his office; but then again, when I started coming to him for therapy I was fourteen. Sometimes when I would get really bored I'd ask good old OWL if we could draw pictures instead of talking. Sometimes he'd say yes to this. Then I'd draw pictures of monsters and say that I wanted to kill myself because my psyche was so tortured by the fact that my mother wrote erotic novels. The truth was far more tragic than that; the truth was my psyche was just very, very bored.

Doctor B was cute, and although she seemed a bit slow, she was the one who ultimately sent me to rehab. Of course that was after months of falling asleep on her sofa. She believed my falling asleep on her sofa was due to what the psychoanalysts call "resistance." The truth was my falling asleep on her sofa had more to do with a little thing called taking a handful of Valium to come down from the coke right before our sessions. Doctor B felt really bad about sending me to rehab. I would have liked her more had she not stumbled into asking me that fatal question: "Do you think your mother's erotic novel writing has been a negative influence in your life?"

Yes, all of these shrinks therapized the overprivileged members of the Upper East Side, but there was one shrink in my life whose breadth was much larger, whose waiting room always looked like the cover of *Us* magazine. That shrink was named Adolf Hitler.

Adolf Hitler was Mom's shrink. I wasn't famous enough to go to Adolf.

Adolf was a tad unconventional. She had written a few books about therapy. She practiced with her husband, who was a former cop. For the sake of discretion we will call him Eva Braun.

Adolf saw her patients in her enormous penthouse apartment in the East Sixties. She lived in the apartment with her husband, Eva Braun, and her housekeeper and her housekeeper's two children, whom she had adopted, but that, dear readers, is where the charity ends.

Mom took me to Adolf for joint sessions to work on our relationship. The first time I went I was nine. I think it's incredibly important to understand how well-adjusted I was. I'd been to every mental health professional in the tristate area, but I was pretty sane. Sure, I hadn't slept through the night since the age of three. What kid does? When my nanny Margaret would tuck me in, I would demand that she check on me every hour for the entire night. I was on the edge of being tossed out of Dalton. At the age of eight I had gone through a period of telling people I was going to sue them. Upon seeing Bela Lugosi's *Dracula* I had become completely obsessed with covering my neck so no one could bite me. I was obsessed with the idea that the Manson family was coming to get me. That obsession only went away last week. So what I'm trying to say is that I was a pretty normal, well-adjusted kid, or at least I wasn't Lizzie Grubman or the girl who murdered the old guy in Central Park.

Adolf would answer the door in a gray paisley muumuu. She had thin, gray hair. She was the opposite of all the earnest shrinks I saw. She was fat, plump, luscious, and gargantuan. She didn't have all those pesky boundaries that the other shrinks had. She always talked about her personal life, often in excruciating detail. She always dropped the names of her famous clients, so that we could know that celebrities are people, too, God damn it! She constantly gave us little tchotchke presents, like pale little porcelain figures and immense pins with rhinestones on them and other creepy things.

As I saw it there were two great things about going to Adolf. One was that she always put out a very nice assortment of cookies. The other was that you almost always saw a famous person in Adolf's waiting room. Sometimes it was a tall blond model (I would guess a non–cookie eater). Sometimes it was a handsome, cleft-chinned Hollywood star with a history of hookers and drugs. Sometimes it was a newscaster with shellacked hair. Whoever it was, it was always someone famous.

At Mom's and my first session together with Adolf, she greeted us at the door. She was wearing the paisley muumuu which she would wear every single subsequent session.

"Darlings! Darlings! Come in!" Adolf embraced me. She was smushy-bodied. Then again, so was I.

"Hello, Adolf, this is my daughter, Molly!"

"Molly darling!! I've heard so much about you!" Adolf embraced me again. Is this what you want your mother's shrink to say about you? What does it mean that she's heard so much about me?

"Hi! It's nice to meet you."

"Yes, darling, wonderful, darling."

"Do you have any cookies? Mom said you have cookies. I like cookies. I don't like Oreos, though."

"Darlings!! Let's go into my office."

"Do you know why I don't like Oreos?"

Adolf led us down a long hallway.

"Because once I ate two boxes of Oreos and then I started puking. Remember that, Mom?"

Mom blushed.

"I puked all day. Then I puked all night."

Mom nodded. We followed. We sat down in Adolf's office. It was nice, if you like paisley wallpaper and paisley pillows.

"Darlings! So tell me, how is everyone today?"

"Do you have any candy?" I asked.

"Ohh, I almost forgot. Mimi! Mimi! MMMMMMimi!" Adolf screamed for her maid.

The skinny, tired Philippine maid wore one of those humiliating white maid's dresses and a little maid's hat. She came in with a huge plate of cookies. I realized I had found my favorite shrink in Manhattan. I realized I was home.

"Is this good, darling?"

"Yes, Dr. Hitler."

"Ohh, don't call me Dr. Hitler, call me Auntie Adolf."

I was a little shocked. I thought you were supposed to call shrinks "Doctor." Even the truly incompetent social worker who opened her mail during our sessions wanted to be called Doctor. "Okay, Auntie Adolf."

"So, Erica, tell me, how are you and Molly doing?"

"Well, I've been trying to talk to Molly about the possibility that I might marry—"

I interjected. "Do you know that Mommy was in *New York Woman* magazine"

Auntie Adolf smiled. "No, I didn't know that."

"My friend Teddy's dad thinks *New York Woman* magazine is going under."

"Kids today!" Hitler laughed, and then she stopped and looked me straight in the eye. "Let's get serious. Do you feel repressed sexually because your mother writes erotic novels? Brilliant, classic, classy novels, but erotic still the same."

"I'm nine."

Hitler looked at me. "I think you're afraid to come clean with us, to be open. Look, I'm a professional. I am the shrink to Famous Actress. I am also the shrink to Famous Actor. I have written four bestselling books; there is nothing that you can't tell Auntie Adolf."

"I don't know what *repressed* means."

"Darling, darling, darling, let's be honest here. You've got a lot of defiance."

"Mom, can we go home?"

"Look, if this is too much emotional work for today, I completely understand. But someday, if you don't confront your difficult relationship with your mother, you'll be forever in its shadow."

"I don't know what that means. I'm missing *Diff'rent Strokes*. I'm missing my shows!"

Mom looked embarrassed.

Auntie Adolf smiled. "We'll talk about this in our next session. By the way, Erica, Famous Actress with Even More Famous Cocaine Problem should be in the waiting room. You should slip her a copy of *Fear of Flying*. She's looking for a strong female lead. I thought of *Fear of Flying* right away. Who owns the rights to that, anyway?"

And so we left Auntie Adolf.

Unfortunately, this session was only the beginning with Auntie Adolf. I think it's important to add a little background information here. Mom loved Auntie Adolf because she was nice. Mom's mom wasn't nice. She was a lot of things. She was interesting. She was a painter. She was beautiful. She supposedly had an IQ of 200. But let's just be honest, Grandma Eda wasn't so nice, and she was nuts. She is famous for such antics as pulling her clothing off on the crosstown bus. She is known for obsessively washing the family dog so many times that it got mange. Lately, of course, Grandma is charming and adorable. But that might be because of Prozac. Anyway, Mom liked Auntie Adolf because she was very loving. And Auntie Adolf liked Mom because she paid in cash and was famous.

The reason Mom was taking me to all these shrinks was because I was fat. Anywhere else in the world, when you are fat, you are exactly that, but here in Manhattan fatness can only be a sign that you are in fact mentally ill.

Our second session focused on fatness. Auntie Adolf answered the door in her signature gray paisley muumuu. She held me to her breast. Mom wore red glasses like Sally Jessy

Raphaël, who was back then (at least it seemed to me) the most famous woman alive.

"Darlings! Let's go into my office. Mimi!!!!!!!! MMMM-MMMimi!!!! Where are the cookies? We need cookies!"

We followed Hitler.

We sat down on the paisley pillows.

"So, Molly, do you feel repressed because your mother writes erotica? Is that fact keeping you from really coming into your own? I think it might be, and if it is I'd like to illustrate a little story from my own life as a way of making you understand just how important it is to seize your life from your famous parent."

"Can I have a cookie?"

"A long time ago, when I was just a young shrink, Famous Actor came to me; this was before he won all those Oscars, mind you. It was before he hit it big. I mean, sure, he was famous then, but he wasn't anywhere as famous as he would be. He came to me because he was obsessed with little boys, and this obsession wasn't helping him with his—"

"Can I have a cookie?"

"Don't you understand, Molly? This is your entire life. This man was able to stop with the little boys and now he's so famous that he can direct. Wouldn't you like to be able to direct?"

"But I'm nine."

"If you don't deal with this now . . . Well, anything could happen. In five years you could be running around with the Symbionese Liberation Party wearing white patent leather boots like Patty Hearst."

"Who's Patty Hearst?"

"That's right, Patty Hearst, and we have to talk about something very very important related to that."

"What?"

"You may not want to talk about this, Molly. It's a very sensitive thing. It's something most people feel embarrassed to talk about, but we must confront this issue if we're going to move forward in your treatment."

"Huh?" I asked.

"Molly," enormous hulking Adolf said to me, "your weight is really a problem."

"Huh?"

"Your mother and I want to get you on a diet. We have found a personal trainer who will work with you."

Mom chimed in. "Honey, I'm just doing this because I love you and I want you to have a normal life. I don't want you to be fat."

"What's a trainer?"

Very fat Auntie Adolf smiled. "A trainer is someone who will get you into shape. Many of my patients have seen trainers; for example, Famous Actress had three trainers. Also Famous Actor has two trainers and three nutritionists and masseurs. He's such a great patient. Of course he has a lot of problems with his mother and the fact that he's a closeted homosexual. *Oops,* his problem is that people are always *saying* that he's a closeted homosexual. That is his problem."

"What's a homosexual?" I was puzzled. "Can I have a cookie?" I looked longingly at the tray of cookies. "Isn't Great-Uncle Shlomo a homosexual?"

"No, darling, that's a homophobic."

"I went on a diet." Auntie Adolf smiled at me.

"That's great."

"Yes, I went on a diet." Enormous Auntie Adolf took a cookie and popped it in her mouth. Her flabby, giant arms flapped against each other.

"Humm," I said.

"Yes, do you want to know what I learned on my diet?"

"No."

"Molly, don't be rude."

"I mean yes."

"Kids today! She really is a pistol."

"I learned to enjoy every single morsel of food. See this caramel?" She held high a piece of caramel. I looked at it lovingly. "This piece of caramel. I will really enjoy this piece of caramel."

Mom looked on, confused.

Adolf put the piece of caramel in her enormous mouth. She sucked on it for what seemed like an hour but was only a minute. She then chewed the caramel and swallowed it. "Do you see how much I enjoyed that piece of caramel?"

Mom looked baffled.

I was puzzled.

"See, I learned that enjoying food is the key to losing weight."

"Ohh," I said.

"See, Molly, that's how you'll lose all the weight so one day you can be a famous actress like my patient Famous Actress, or maybe you'll just be thin so you can marry someone like my other favorite patient, Famous Actor."

"Mom, can we go home now? It's four o'clock and I'm missing my favorite shows. I'm missing *The Facts of Life.*"

"Hon, not just yet."

"Pllllllllllllllllllllllllllease," I said, and then I broke into singing the *Facts of Life* theme song,

You take the good, you take the bad,
you take them both and there you have
the facts of life, the facts of life. Ohh, the facts of life.

"Look." Adolf pushed her gray, stringy hair behind her ears. "Look, Molly. I don't want to scare you, but I had a patient, Very Famous Actor, who had a famous father. He was a brilliant actor. I mean, yes, he had his problems with the women. He had several illegitimate children, but of course they were all born to mothers that were supermodels. These children were so incredible looking. Of course they were very screwed-up kids in my professional opinion. But that, darling Molly, is beside the point. Your mother is a very brilliant writer. You know that, don't you? And if you don't confront her being the zeitgeist of the culture, well, then you'll be doomed to be just like this man. Did you know that that famous actor has been in rehab fourteen times? And don't forget the illegitimate children. You don't want to have illegitimate children, do you?"

"I don't know what illegitimate children are. I'm nine."

"Sometimes being the son of the man who created Hollywood, fabulously wealthy, insanely talented, and gorgeous isn't enough," Hitler said. "Sometimes the superstar inside just needs a hug."

"Look, I'll hug my inner superstar, whatever. But Mom, I'm missing *The Facts of Life*. Can we go home? I really want to see *The Facts of Life*. Plllllleeeeeease!"

Mom looked at Hitler. "Is it okay if I take her home?"

"Sure, Erica, darling," Hitler said, smiling. "But let me just ask Molly one last thing, which is, don't you think that admitting your mother's erotic novels have repressed you will set you free?"

"I don't know what you're talking about."

Hitler looked at me for a long minute. "You know my patients are all famous. Sure, not all of them are as famous as Famous Actor, sure not all of them are as rich as Famous Rich Actor, but my patients are very, very, very famous. And you know what, Molly?"

"Can I go home?"

"Do you know what, Molly?"

"What?"

"They aren't that happy. I mean, sure, Famous Actor would be happier if he didn't have to always hide the fact that he has herpes. But basically zillions of dollars, millions of groupies, several platinum albums, and endless appearances on the cover of *Vogue* magazine won't be able to solve your problems, you understand that?"

"Yes, Auntie Adolf. Can I go home and watch my shows?"

And so I went home and watched my shows. Mom continued to see Hitler until she wrote that Eva Braun used to fall asleep during the group sessions that he and Hitler would run. Then Hitler was mad at Mom and stopped treating her. As soon as Mom's treatment with Hitler was over, Mom suddenly got much weller. This led us to believe that Mom's new shrink was a miracle worker, or perhaps that Hitler wasn't that great a shrink.

Great shrink or no, Auntie Adolf taught me everything I ever needed to know about life. She was my Henry Kissinger. She taught me the truly important things, like that Famous Actor has herpes. And Famous Actress is a real hard-core sex addict, which is why she always has to sleep with her directors. Yes, I received many gifts from Auntie Adolf, none of which I can think of right now. Maybe, if Mom had been as famous as Susan Lucci, then I would have gotten better therapy from Adolf, but regardless, I think it's fair to say that I wouldn't be the woman I am today if it weren't for the love and nurturing and connections I received from Adolf Hitler.

mom's fourth chance at happiness

✻

WHEN I MET KEN, I thought he was a dork. He came over to the town house with the hot pink door on Ninety-fourth Street. Like all of Mom's suitors, he understood the truly important things in life, like the importance of bringing me presents, but poor Ken was childless, a divorce lawyer to boot, and did not know toys. He also did not know multicolored chocolate taste tests like Mom's last boyfriend, a southern gentleman more interested in being a dad than in being a husband. Ken also didn't know Chocolate Soup (the cool store on Madison Ave. that sold hundred-dollar book bags) or chocolate Easter baskets. All Ken knew was that he loved France. So Ken brought me back some pens from France that were in the colors of the French flag. He also brought me back a sweatshirt in the colors of the French flag.

Pandora's box was opened when Mom and Ken were fixed up on a blind date. She was at the time driving a red

Jaguar (which I later totaled). Because she was a little near-sighted, she almost hit him with the Jaguar. At that moment he knew he had found a woman who was a worse driver than he was, which was not an easy thing to find. What made him sure of this was her confession that she couldn't exactly see after dark due to night blindness. And so it was a perfect pairing: he would drive in both lanes on the highway and she wouldn't be able to complain 'cause she couldn't see what he was doing.

There was only one problem: me. I liked the southern gentleman who brought me chocolate. I didn't like Ken, who brought me French pens. Like Donald Rumsfeld, I hated France. I hated pens. I hated Ken. Luckily, I was no shrinking violet, no wallflower, so one night at dinner, seated at the large round wooden dining-room table, I came right out and told him. We were eating pasta—Ken, Mom, my nanny Margaret, and I. I had just spilled pasta sauce all over myself.

"So your mother and I would like to take you to France with us this summer. Would you like that?"

"Like you? I've never liked you."

It was a cold day in May. Mom laughed. "Kids today. She's in therapy three times a week. It's really helping her." Margaret grimaced.

I smiled my best evil smile. "In fact, you disgust me!"

"MOLLY!" Margaret screamed.

Mom laughed nervously. "She's under a lot of stress. She's just doing this thing the shrinks say—"

"I've never liked you. You're a bastard, just like your father! He was a bastard too!"

"That's it! Someone's going to their room right now!" Margaret looked tired.

"But why?" I started crying.

"Because we don't call people bastards." Margaret looked very tired.

"But . . ."

"To your room."

Ken did not like being called a bastard. But I felt good about telling him how I felt, until Margaret informed me that my performance had won me the privilege of no dessert.

Let me just shine a tiny bit of light on the inner workings of my psyche—back then my role model for all human interaction was Alexis Carrington. The "across the face slap" and the "Like you? I've NEVER liked you. In fact you DISGUST me" were the Alexis Carrington moves I used most; when I was twelve years old, they were my signature moves.

There were only two problems with this. Problem 1 was that I felt I might have irreparably damaged Ken's feelings (I guess I forgot he was a divorce lawyer and people said stuff like that to him every day). And problem 2 (my much larger problem) was that after three whole months of dating, Ken had asked Mom to marry him and she had said yes.

This was not good. I had not planned on this.

A few days later I was sitting in Westport in the haunted, creepy house I grew up in (a house chock-full of Manson family members hiding in every cupboard). "I have to show you something," Mom said.

Ohh goody, I thought, Mom's bought me a present. She shouldn't have. Well, yes she should have. But what had she bought me? Was it chocolate? Or was it something better? Perhaps a giant stuffed animal that talked and played video games? Or perhaps another pony?

"Look." We were sitting in her giant, sun-filled office, at her wooden desk, looking out at her enormous eighties-style computer, and all the trees, bugs, and ticks of Connecticut.

"What are those, Mom?" They were not presents, they came in a box but they were not presents, not chocolate, not cookies, not a giant stuffed bear that also spoke French. They were wedding invitations; my mother was trying to show me invitations to her fourth wedding. This I did not like. I wanted chocolate. I wanted her to give up and dedicate the rest of her life to her true purpose—entertaining and shopping for her little girl.

The invitations were nice enough; they said the usual blah-blah-blah thing. They seemed okay. Stamped across them in red ink was "A triumph of hope over experience."

"See, they're funny." She smiled. Mom was happy. She had found love. What had I found? Nothing except French pens.

"There is nothing funny about this," I said and then walked out of the room like Alexis Carrington. This was not "a triumph of hope over experience." This was my worst nightmare.

When you're twelve, there is nothing funny about your mother's fourth wedding. I'd already been in my father's wedding, and I hadn't been thrilled with the results: two little brothers (whom I now love more than anything in the world and live for, but whom I wasn't so happy with back then, because they were cute and got presents). I was smart. I had already been kicked out of one of the finest schools in the country. I understood what a wedding meant. I got it. I knew it would be only a few months before little replacement children were moving into my room and trying to play with my toys.

A mere month later we were driving to Vermont, to the condo my stepfather owned in Warren, Vermont. Margaret was touched that Mom was getting yet another chance at love. Personally, I felt you should only get three chances at the institution of marriage, and after that you had to stay with my father.

We drove and drove and drove and drove. And then, in the time it takes to get to Europe, we were in Vermont. We settled in at the condo before we went off to the rehearsal dinner. It was summer. It was beautiful. Everybody was happy. Everybody but me.

Ken's parents threw the rehearsal dinner at a restaurant that had a magician. It was nice. There was a lot of food. I ate till I hallucinated, and then Mom said she'd drive me back to the condo. Now I had learned two very important lessons from my childhood—one was never get in a car with Grandpa Howie, and the other was never get in a car with Mom after dark because her eyes, as I noted previously, have plenty of cones for checking out Fendi handbags during the day but not enough rods to distinguish between the road and the trees at night. So, I jumped in the car and Mom revved up the engine and after a mere five miles we got horribly and irrevocably lost.

Mom got really, really mad. She said, "That bastard, I'm not going to marry him." I agreed. After all, he had no part in getting us lost, but he was a man, and a man who liked France. Mom yelled and screamed. "He's an asshole." A summer thunderstorm clapped over our heads.

I agreed. "And he brought me pens, that bastard. What a bastard he is!"

"I'm not going to marry him. This has been a terrible mistake."

"I couldn't agree more."

"That's it."

"YES!! It is. Dump him, Mom!"

"Yes . . . But I love him."

"Gross."

Miraculously, at that moment we found our way to the condo. And at that moment Mom decided Ken wasn't so bad after all. And at that moment, I realized this wedding was a go whether I got on board or not. So in typical Molly fashion, I did not get on board.

The next day the parking lot outside the condo was all decked out in the finest country condo style. A huge yellow tent covered the lot. A wooden dance floor gleamed on the gravel ground. Mom wore a red silk dress that Koos had made. Ken wore a suit. Margaret wore lavender. I wore a frown. A string quartet played classical music. A chocolate wedding cake sat waiting to be eaten. Chocolate-covered strawberries were passed on silver platters. Bartenders tended bar. Various people sipped drinks and gossiped. You could almost forget you were in a parking lot.

And then the wedding began. Everyone sat in rows of chairs. I was the flower girl, so I walked down the aisle before my mom. I had also been the flower girl at my father's wedding. Mom read a truly distressing poem about a horny Boy Scout and a private plane. I covered my ears and tried to calm myself by thinking about the chocolate-covered strawberries

I'd gorge myself on later. To this day I am wildly embarrassed by Mom's dirty poems, and more interestingly, I still love chocolate strawberries.

Many long speeches were read, many long poems were recited, and then, in the time it takes to get to Madagascar from Newark by large, leaking ferryboat operated by blind, indigent white-tailed deer, it was over and I had a stepfather.

There was much celebrating. Mom was so happy. Ken was thrilled. Even Margaret cried with joy. The only person who wasn't happy was me.

Soon after, Mom and Ken went on a very long honeymoon. When they came back we moved from the town house to the Imperial House, a white-brick building in the Sixties on the Upper East Side. The Imperial House had been a refuge for gay couples who couldn't get past the more stodgy boards on Park, Madison, and Fifth Avenues. It was a nice building run by Irish doormen, but I hated living there because I hated Mom's fourth chance at happiness.

But as with all things, after a while I got used to it. I stopped being twelve and started being thirteen and then fourteen. At fourteen I was thrilled that Mom had someone to keep her occupied and out of the house. After all, you can't have the drug dealer come to the house unless your mom's out (well, you can, but that's another story). "Look, Mom, everybody has friends in their forties named Felix who are from Ecuador and have tattoos that say 'Krazy-eyed-killer' on their hands." I got used to the apartment. I got used to the stepfather. I got used to the Imperial House. I got into drugs.

In the morning Mom's fourth chance at happiness and I would eat breakfast together. He'd read the *Times* and I'd read what all high school kids read: Page Six of the *New York Post*. Sometimes we'd fight. Sometimes we'd say nothing to each other. Then I would smoke five cigarettes while waiting for the school bus, then I would get to school in Riverdale and sneak into the bushes, where I would smoke another five cigarettes before class, then I would go to class, then after class I would sneak back into the bushes to smoke another five cigarettes. After school I would come home, not eat, smoke, and go to the gym, then later I would smoke more and then possibly smoke some pot, all the while trying to ignore the roll of uncooked cookie dough which I would eventually eat. High school was for me truly a high.

I then failed out of many colleges, graduated from an illustrious rehab facility, and began an adult life of abstinence from drugs and alcohol but not cigarettes—that came later. I came home to live and eat huge cinnamon buns. It was then that I learned just how much I loved my mom's fourth chance at happiness, Mr. Ken Burrows, Esq.

I wasn't living with them anymore (do not confuse this with not living *off* them, I was in fact still living off them). I had moved into another apartment in the same building. It was a Monday morning, and I was oversleeping. I took a shower. Then when I got out of the shower I called Mom to see if she wanted to fight with me that sunny Monday morning. Only Mom couldn't fight with me because she wasn't there. Carmen, the world's nicest housekeeper, answered the phone.

"Mister Burroo not here. He at the hospital."

Ken had stepped into the elevator and had to be carried out. He thought he was having a heart attack. Matthew, the

Irish doorman, had called an ambulance for him. He went to New York Hospital.

I put on a fashionable outfit (come on, there're single doctors there) and jumped in a taxi and headed out for New York Hospital. When I got there the doctor told us everything was fine. That Ken had actually had the best kind of heart attack and he would be out playing golf (or in the case of a divorce lawyer, yelling at people) within the next week. I was sent home to pick up a suitable outfit for Mom to wear in the hospital while she waited for Ken to get cured.

I picked some lovely Missoni knits. I felt that the striped bright colors said, I'm alive and yet I'm also concerned.

I got into another cab and headed the four blocks back to New York Hospital. Unfortunately, when I got there I got bad news. The cheery doctor had been wrong about this best kind of heart attack shtick. The truth was Ken was having a very serious aneurysm and was going to have to have emergency surgery.

Mom and I went in to see Ken before the surgery. They were bringing his body temperature down so that they could operate on him. His hands were freezing cold. For the first time ever, Ken looked very scared. Mom was scared. I was also scared. Even the doctors looked scared.

"If I don't make it, will you take care of my other step-daughter?"

What could I say? "Of course I will look out for her."

He gave me a hug, and then I left him and Mom to say their good-byes.

Mom and I sat in the waiting room of New York Hospital. Gerry, Mom's best friend, sat with us. We read magazines.

We ate hospital food. We made jokes. We watched *Days of Our Lives* with the sound off. But mostly we just worried. It was a long day. At the end of it the doctor came out and told us the operation had been a success, although there were of course many more hurdles to go over before he got completely better. But Ken's heart was no longer in danger of exploding.

We were ecstatic. We went into the cardiac ICU to see him. He didn't look like his operation had been a success. He was bluish from being frozen. He was breathing with the help of a respirator, and he was unconscious. But we took the doctor's word and went home.

Horrible things have a way of making the members of my family abnormally sane. Mom and I went home, ordered pizza, and watched TV. I stayed in her house during the time Ken was in the hospital. We watched TV in the sane eye of what was otherwise a hurricane of craziness.

Of course I was consumed with the poor me's. Which is not that unusual for me. I felt as if we were now the kind of people whom others felt bad for. I felt as if we were a tragic family. What I didn't understand was that actually what we were living was just par for the course. What New York City divorce lawyer doesn't have a massive aneurysm? Might I be so bold as to suggest to those folks at New York Hospital that they might rename the Coronary Care Unit "the unit that an absence of prenups built," or perhaps "the unit that sleeping with your secretary built"?

Anyway, that night Mom and I slept in the same bed. We watched TV. We ate ice cream late into the night. When I was a little kid living in the house with the hot pink door on

Ninety-fourth street, Mom would come into my bedroom late at night and ask me if I wanted to go into her room and watch *The Tonight Show* and eat ice cream. Some of my happiest childhood memories were of eating ice cream and watching *The Tonight Show* with my mom late at night, in a bed that was covered in peach-colored sheets. Sometimes it disturbs me that I associate happiness with Johnny Carson. Sometimes that same fact comforts me.

Sometimes I wonder how we lived though those weeks Ken spent in the cardiac ICU. Sometimes I think that it never happened. But then I hug Ken and can feel the square box that lies just under the skin right about where the shirt pocket is, or I get Ken really stressed out (like with my wedding), and then his pacemaker goes off.

When I did drugs (please note: these next few lines could be either fascinating or perhaps woefully self-indulgent; if it's the latter just don't post that in your review on www.amazon.com, 'cause then I'll be sad, but not too sad to find you and stalk you, although sad all the same), I did them on some level as a way of stealing my life back from my famous mother. I wanted my life to be about me. I wanted everything to be about me. I was only able to achieve that level of self-centeredness through drugs and alcohol. When Ken got sick I was able to shed some of the selfishness that plagues me. When Ken got sick I was able to be there for Mom. When Ken got sick I was able to see that I hadn't needed to steal my life, it had been mine all along; I just hadn't seen it that way.

I had never voted for Ken. I liked the southern gentleman. I also liked the alcoholic wine dealer who ended up in jail (but only after he dated the Mayflower Madam). I liked the sort-of-married Venetian. I liked the fat guy who slept in a single bed with his daughter. I liked all the scumbags. That is because I have very, very, very bad judgment.

Ultimately I learned the greatest lesson ever from my stepfather, a lesson that will forever change my life, a lesson I am grateful to know. I learned that there's a very good reason why moms don't let their twelve-year-old daughters pick their husbands. And who knows more about picking a compatible mate than a divorce lawyer?

my new daddy is a jailbird or
perhaps an italian playboy

*

I FEEL THAT I HAVEN'T given a fair shake to all the other men along the way who could have been my new daddy. Speaking as an erotic memoirist for a moment, I think that each of these men affected me in very different and very meaningful ways. For example, I don't think I would have developed a love for baby back ribs if it hadn't been for Mr. Pig. I never would have seen Venice quite so many times if it hadn't been for the Italian playboy. You see, dear reader, being a stepfather is a very serious and important job; Mom was even engaged to one of these men. These are potential dads who did not merit their own essays but who are beautiful and special people all the same.

It was the eighties when a wine dealer named Zachy (a funny guy from Scarsdale) introduced Mom to the man we will call (for the usual purpose of not getting sued) Mr. Pig. I have chosen this name because someone much more successful than I am has already taken the name Mr. Big.

Mr. Pig drove an enormous BMW. He had a daughter who was a few years older than me. She was a tad zany. You know the type: therapy since she was three, poorly adjusted, somewhat bratty, student at the Dalton School (oh wait, that also describes me). Mr. Pig was, like Zachy, a wine dealer. He liked golf, wine, golf, wine, and also, for the sake of variety, food, especially ribs. Needless to say, Mr. Pig was fat, not in the sexy way Mr. Big is fat but more in a generally nonsexy fat way. I liked Mr. Pig. He took me to Rusty Staub's ribs restaurant. We ate ribs like pigs (is that cannibalism?).

Mr. Pig also took us to Hilton Head to go golfing. He bought my mom a little model of an Aston Martin. He said he'd buy her a real one one day. But he never did because he found himself very busy in jail—but I'm getting ahead of myself. Mom and Mr. Pig were happy. Mom and Mr. Pig got engaged. We spent Christmas with Mr. Pig. Of course we're Jewish. Mr. Pig was Jewish. His whole family was Jewish. And yet, puzzlingly enough, both of our families celebrated the birth of Jesus. Maybe if Neiman Marcus had made a Chanukah book filled with Chanukah houses, Chanukah trees, and Jewish Santas, our lives would be different. The following is an accurate retelling of what happened:

Mr. Pig drove us into Manhattan in his huge gas-guzzling BMW. He took us to his sister's house on the Upper West Side. The party was festive but became much, much more festive when I got into the peanut-butter rum balls. I ate twenty of them. I didn't understand then what I understand now, having graduated from an illustrious rehab facility: these rum balls were the marriage of my two favorite things, food and booze. Of course I was eleven then, so I didn't yet know that I loved booze.

Mom looked at me. I was green. "Are you okay?"

"I think I ate too many of those chocolate–peanut-butter balls."

Mom turned to Mr. Pig's sister. "Those weren't rum balls, were they?"

Mr. Pig's sister turned to Mom. "Yes, they were. They're a family recipe, it was Great-Grandma who first started making them. They're my legacy. They're all I have to remember my dear, sweet grandmother."

"Mommy, I think I'm gonna throw up."

"Oh honey, it's okay. If you need to puke, puke."

Mr. Pig's sister screamed, "Oh dear God! Not in the living room, you little brat, I just got this new white suede sofa."

"Don't you dare scream at my daughter after you fed her rum balls. You're like a pusher. It's your fault if she throws up," Mom said.

Needless to say, chaos ensued.

I didn't puke on her sofa, but I felt pretty crappy on the drive home, and I don't think I'll ever eat peanut-butter-rum balls again.

But luckily, that didn't break up Mom and Mr. Pig. In fact, soon afterward Mr. Pig decided that he was going to build Mom her own building on his property in Westchester. It was a three-story building. The basement would be an exercise studio. The second floor would have a big room for Mom to hang out in, and the third floor would be Mom's office. The only problem was that there were no windows in this building. Mr. Pig was about to build Mom an office with no windows. Was this a sign of a larger problem in their relationship?

Mom would say yes. Soon afterward, they broke up. Maybe there was more to it than just the windowless office; maybe Mom realized that Mr. Pig was exactly that. Of course Mr. Pig was upset. Mom was upset. But in his distress Mr. Pig was able to find comfort in the arms of the Mayflower Madam, an eighties celebrity known by the IRS and her parents as Ms. Sidney Biddle Barrows. It turns out that Mr. Pig was an intellectual. Mom wasn't the only writer in the world. Mr. Pig was able to find someone else who loved letters the way he did: Ms. Biddle Barrows, author of *Just Between Us Girls: Secrets About Men from the Madam Who Knows.*

A few years later Mom found comfort in the fact that Mr. Pig went to jail for the hundreds of bottles of wine he was hiding under the Thames River. He seemed to have neglected to pay the IRS a substantial sum of money. This jail thing made Mom realize that a windowless office would have only been the beginning of much, much larger problems with Mr. Pig, who now resides in a different kind of windowless room.

So Mom found comfort in the arms of a genuine Italian playboy. She met him in Venice, the land of people who don't work. He had gray, curly hair and blue eyes. He also had a wife. But his wife was both very old and very fat; he swore they no longer slept in the same bed.

"You see, she is very, very rich. She owns the hundreds of miles of incredibly valuable land that surround Venice, otherwise known as the Veneto," the Italian playboy explained to Mom when she asked why he stayed with her if they didn't sleep in the same bed.

Mom and the playboy had good times. Their relationship was a true meeting of the minds. They studied physics together. They read the work of Proust together. They entertained different theories about cold-water fusion together. They talked about the future of the Middle East. They wondered how to fix Cuba. They taught each other Sanskrit. Mom rented a house in Venice right near the playboy, so that they could continue their studying together. Ah, Sanskrit, the language of love, or at least a language that is very hard to read.

The playboy's wife really liked Mom. She was no fool. She understood what was going on with her dim-witted but hot husband. And she realized that Mom was an excellent person to ask to host boring charity events filled with old people, and that is exactly what she did. Because before being the wife of a playboy, or the owner of the Veneto, or the fat duchess, she was a Venetian, and along with being a Venetian comes the relentless quest for free stuff.

The fat duchess realized the advantages of her situation and was able to get Mom to help her sons publish their novels. The fat duchess knew how to play it. And one might even say that the fat duchess got the most out of the relationship.

Mom and the playboy continued. We would come to Venice for the summers. He'd drop by for a coffee or a weekend. He had a boat that made me like him. Sometimes he'd take us to the neighboring islands on his boat. I liked that a lot. Water taxis cost seventy-five to eighty dollars per trip, so in many ways the playboy was really just all about altruism. In many ways this man was obsessed with helping a young erotic writer and single mom manage her life and raise her child.

Speaking of helpful, once we got locked out of the incredibly creepy house we were renting, a house that was filled with creepy paintings with eyes that followed you around the room and scary racist sculptures of slave boys holding lanterns. The playboy came to the rescue. The playboy called the police. Quite unexpectedly, the police came. Then the playboy decided he had done enough good deeds for the day and went home to bed.

"The police will handle this, Erica. I am tired."

"Are you sure we shouldn't have just called the locksmith?"

He laughed and laughed and laughed and laughed. "What are you, crazy? This is Venice. You call the locksmith, he shows up at your door drunk in three months."

"But the police."

He laughed and laughed. He knew perfect English—he had learned it when he was a kid—but he spoke in a fragmented way anyway. "Errrriccaaa, stop worry. Police will take care. Call me tomorrow. I must make way home to my wife."

The police were able to open the door for us. We kind of looked like idiots for calling the police, but the police found the whole incident very amusing. They had many, many laughs at the hysterical American women.

We had good times with the playboy, good times indeed. But nothing with a married Italian playboy is forever. I think there is only so much Sanskrit one woman can learn. A mere five years later Mom finally broke it off with the playboy upon meeting the divorce lawyer who would become her husband.

But let's not skip the others along the way. For example, there was the southern gentleman who did chocolate taste tests with me. You see, in Venice they had this multicolored chocolate, and the southern gentleman and I would always wonder whether differently colored chocolates tasted different. Did the green chocolate taste different than the pink, or did the brown chocolate taste different than the yellow? The southern gentleman and I did a true blindfolded taste test (remember this was the eighties, you couldn't turn on a TV without seeing some kind of blindfolded taste test for Coke vs. Pepsi or something). Of course in the end I decided the flavor that tasted best was all of them.

I loved the southern gentleman; he was so weird. He was also so cheap. When he would travel with us, he'd stay in the cheaper hotel behind the hotel where we'd stay. He took the bus to the airport. I thought that was cool. He was an architect who lived in North Carolina.

Years later he took Mom and me to lunch in a fancy restaurant. He wore funny glasses. He had never married. I was a grown-up.

"So, how are you doing?" Mom said.

"Great. I'm designing many buildings, and I'm dating this fantastic woman."

"Wow, that's great," I said, looking at my rubber chicken.

"Yes, she's wonderful."

"I'm so happy you're happy," Mom said.

"Where is she from?" I asked.

"North Carolina."

"So what does she do?" I asked.

"She's a sword swallower."

"No, she's not." I laughed. The southern gentleman was always a joker.

"Yes, she is."

I laughed and laughed and laughed. Then I said: "That's funny. I'm actually dating Ted Kaczynski. You might have heard of him. He's a big celebrity. You might know him as the Unabomber." I was kidding, sort of.

"No, she really is, a real sword swallower. She swallows swords, for a living."

"Oh, how very unconventional."

"Yes," I agreed. "Very unconventional."

He was the man who was just too weird to date. But we still love him, and Mom and I both hope very much that he found love with the sword swallower.

Then there was Mom's married depressed guy. Now let's be honest here, we've all been with married guys. Even I, a person of alarmingly high moral stature (or something). I was with (when I was in high school) the married fashion designer until he dumped me by having sex with all of my friends and also the girl who worked at the video store.

But Mom's married guy was actually at the time separated (all married guys claim to be separated). I really liked Mom's married guy. He was very smart and cool. He looked and acted like John Cleese except without the famous part. He published a novel that no one ever read or even heard about. He was so depressed. Was he depressed because no one ever read his novel or because he was getting divorced or because he looked like John Cleese and yet wasn't famous? I don't know. Whatever the reason, the married depressed guy had an alarmingly good sense of humor.

He'd come by the house. Mom, Margaret, and I would sit and have pasta dinner with him. (See, Mom knew something the masses didn't. She knew the zeitgeist. Hell, she dated the zeitgeist.) Mom understood there was a totally untapped market of men out there: who needed dates. Mom had stumbled across the Rosetta stone of dating, the answer to her problems: the mentally ill man.

The depressed married guy was basically plucked right out of a Woody Allen movie. He had gray hair. He was prone to complaining. He had nervous twitches all over his body. In many ways he was a lot like me. Now that I think about it, maybe the depressed married guy was my real father. After all, I met him when I was ten, so the chances are good. Now lots of things are starting to make sense! Eureka! If you are reading this, depressed married guy, please e-mail me. We can play catch in the park. You can teach me how to ride a bike.

Mom and I and Margaret had dinner with him one night in our blue dining room (Mom had wanted the dining room to be pink like all the other rooms in the house, but since it had originally been dark green, the lightest color we could paint over it was light blue) in our weird house (which was broken into almost every day) with the hot pink door on Ninety-fourth Street.

"How are you doing, Depressed Married Guy?" Margaret would ask while putting butter on my pasta.

"Well, I'm wondering what's the point of going on. It's all so meaningless. I thought publishing a book would give my life meaning. I thought publishing a book would make the universe make sense. But the truth is that someday we're all going to die and then we'll be dead. I often wonder how can we go on living day to day when we could be—"

"You know . . ." Mom smiled at the depressed married guy.

"Yes, but is that enough? We could all be dead tomorrow."

"Not in front of the kiddie, she's already in therapy three times a week." Mom smiled. "Mommy loves you and isn't going to be dead tomorrow, honey."

"But don't you understand, Erica? This is about so much more than therapy. And sure, aren't we all in therapy three times a week? I say you're doing something right if she's in therapy three times a week. I say that's a sign of some good parenting."

"I hate Doctor A! She's a bitch."

"Don't say that word," Margaret said, her blood pressure rising.

"What word?"

"You know what word."

The depressed married guy continued. "This is about something larger, more infinite. Come on, look around you—here we are in this huge universe. We're just a tiny dot."

"Doctor A is a bitch!"

"Don't say *bitch*. That's not a nice word." Margaret looked tired. She hadn't actually taken a vacation (or any time without me) since 'eighty-one, and it was now 'eighty-eight.

"Why? YOU just did."

"Can't you see how meaningless it all is? We're just a dot."

"Look, you just said *bitch*! Why can't I say it? You just said it. It's not fair that you can say *bitch* and I can't say *bitch*. After all, we know a bitch is just a female dog."

Margaret was visibly annoyed. The depressed married guy looked depressed. Mom smiled warily and asked, "Could you just not say *bitch*?"

"I'm going to have to hit you with a wooden spoon." This was Margaret's favorite threat, although she only ever did it once and ultimately I found the whole experience oddly painless.

"Can I have ice cream?"

"Not until you finish dinner."

"PLLLLLEASE!!!"

"See, Erica, we're a tiny dot. We're some other universe's excrement. We're just nothing, all of us nothing."

"PPLLLEASE, can I get ice cream?"

"We're all just nothing. We're all just a tiny dot. I think I have to go. I think I'm having a panic attack."

"But?"

"ICE CREAM! I WANT ICE CREAM."

"Is it hot in here? It's hot in here. I have to get out of here. I'm definitely having a panic attack."

And then he ran out the door. That was the last we saw of the depressed married guy. Maybe Mom hadn't stumbled on a brilliant life strategy with the depressed married guy. Maybe dating the mentally ill is a sticky wicket after all.

Then there was the *Artforum* editor. He was Italian. He was the hippest man who ever lived, like an Italian Elvis except with a more decorous set of dance moves. He took

Mom to Nells, where they danced on tables. He called her Air-Re-KAH.

"Ciao, Air-Re-KAH! Let us go down to Save the Robots. We can hang out with the Pet Shop Boys! We can then go over to Bianca's house and party like it is nineteen ninety-nine."

Needless to say, Mom was hip. After all, she lived in a crumbling town house with a pink door—occupied by two sex doctors in the basement and a psychotic secretary upstairs. Mr. *Artforum* was hopelessly hip. He moved back to Rome and married a German princess; they had three children and then got divorced. He and Mom are still great friends.

The following paragraph should be sung:

There were others along the way, bankers and bakers, doctors and dilettantes, writers and reapers, wine dealers and street sweepers, but these are a few of my favorite men, la la la. When the phone rings. When the door clicks. That's when I think of these men. When there is frantic knocking on the door, when a meat truck arrives in our driveway; that's when I think of these men. Yes, these are a few of my favorite men, la la la.

Of course these men taught me everything I ever needed to know about life, like Morrie from *Tuesdays with Morrie* except without the meaningful exchanges or the great life lessons. Mr. Pig taught me about ribs. He taught me about BBQ sauce. He taught me about cholesterol. The southern gentleman taught me about taste tests and their ultimate fallibility. The married depressed guy taught me that the universe was getting larger and larger and one day the whole thing would just swallow us all up. The Italian playboy taught me about boating. The *Artforum* man taught me about Studio 54, the harmonious music of Phil Collins, and the importance of wearing neon. These men were like fathers to me.

Throughout the eighties Mom was finding herself. Her mad dating made it possible for me to get married at a very young age and still know what's out there (basically a lot of married guys, a few gay but closeted guys, a bunch of guys who have problems with commitment, and some guys who are just weird). I learned many things from my mother's dating life. I learned that you should never date actors who end up selling meat from a truck. I learned that sometimes a rich wine dealer is guilty of more than just a criminally bad sense of style; sometimes he is in fact a criminal. I learned that severely depressed married men do not make good boyfriends. I learned that *Artforum* is an illustrious publication. I learned that Italian playboys' wives will screw you more thoroughly than their husbands will. And the number-one thing I learned from my mother's dating was Never date a man who has either of the following going for him: has more than one personality or is currently receiving electroshock treatment.

my brief life with a model

※

THERE WAS A TIME when she was not ninety feet tall lying on a billboard, ruling Times Square like Stalin in a bra and panties. Sometimes it's hard for me to believe that there was a time when she didn't stand larger than most buildings. There was a time when she didn't writhe naked for Yves Saint Laurent's Opium perfume on a bed of velvet pillows, covered only by strappy gold sandals and green eye shadow.

It was the first day of seventh grade, and we were all standing around the Day School gym. From the first second I saw her I knew that I had to be friends with her. You see, I am very very, very, very superficial. I am also very vain, self-centered, self-loathing, self-obsessed, self-effacing, and shallow.

I had no friends. I was hated. I was a dork. Celia Peters and the gymnastic girls called me fat. Part of the reason they called me this was because I was enormously husky, robust, and voluptuous, and had more rolls than a lot of bakeries. My unpopularity was due to the fact that I was a helpless tattletale, a mean brat, a crier, and most offensive of all, a new student at the Day School (I'd been there only since fourth grade; everyone else had been there since Franco ruled Spain).

Sophie Dahl stood in the gym next to me. She was the most beautiful girl I had ever seen in my life. She was taller than all the other seventh graders, boys and girls. She pushed her long, thick yellow hair behind her ears, revealing her soft, white skin and alarmingly steep cheekbones. I had forty bug bites on my calves from mucking stalls at horrible horseback riding camp. She wore a yellow crocheted cotton sweater and a matching miniskirt. She had thin, long, bony legs that swelled with huge knots of knees. I was standing alone against the padded gym walls. The whole room smelled of plastic gym balls, a distinct and very nauseating smell that I can still conjure up even now. Who knew that years later I'd attend numerous self-help meetings in this very gym?

The gymnastics girls, a pack of popular, pretty, prepubescent, plastic princesses, were talking about J. Crew bikinis they had worn that summer. Elizabeth and Stephanie (the brainy girls) were talking about the politics of Eastern Europe. Some of the boys were talking about the band they were starting. No one was talking to Sophie. I saw my moment.

"I'm Molly Jong-Fast. Are you English?"

"Yes," Sophie said.

"Do you know my friend Sam? He's English too. My mom's famous. Did you know that? I've been to England four times. I've been on the Concorde too. Sometimes I go with Mom on book tours. Do you know who my mom is?" Wait, you say. The narrator would never really say something like this, surely not. Well, tragically, ladies and gentlemen, this is exactly what I did say. Now perhaps you can start to understand why my classmates loathed me.

We were both important thirteen-year-olds. Not since Napoleon had met Czar Alexander at the opening of the first Russian Toys "R" Us store had two such luminaries made acquaintance. Not since Carl Gustav Jung met a man named Sigmund has history witnessed such a meeting of the minds.

Sophie Dahl also made me understand another important, inalienable truth, which was that I was going to have to kill myself. I looked at her beautiful, buxom Britishness and understood that if I was gonna have to compete with girls like that, I was in a lot of trouble.

I said I was fat, but I'm not really painting a fair picture of me in all my seventh-grade glory. My hormones were exploding; my face was a war zone. My teeth were jagged, yellow pegs. My skin was red from failed acne treatments, and I had feathered hair and a perm. All of that perfection was wrapped in teal, pink, and magenta polyester sweat suits that my nanny Margaret had bought for me at Alexander's. Odds were good I wasn't going to end up on the cover of *Seventeen* any time soon.

The same could not be said of Sophie. Sophie wore designer clothes. She had a British accent. She lived in an enormous limestone town house on East Seventy-first Street, filled with amazing furniture. Sophie's mother slept on a giant iron bed decorated with iron roses. She had been a model. Pictures of her on the covers of magazines graced the guest bathroom walls. My mother was a feminist. Pictures of my mother constantly appeared in *Spy* magazine and the inky, small-print

New York Times. Sophie's grandpa was Roald Dahl, beloved
children's book author. My grandpa was some guy who was a
Communist and went to jail.

By far Sophie's worst offense was her insane niceness. She
was the nicest person alive. She was Disney movie nice. She
never made fun of anyone. She fed small animals. She didn't
set fire to homeless people. She never stole money from her
parents' domestic help knowing that they wouldn't complain
for fear of getting fired. She never strangled anyone in Central Park during rough sex. She never traded blow jobs for the
crack rock. She never shoplifted, not even from Scoop (a
store on the Upper East Side where shoplifting might actually
be looked on as a public service). Needless to say, she didn't
fare so well at the Day School, the juggernaut of meanness on
the Upper East Side, where the gymnastics girls ruled the
school with an iron leotard and those who couldn't climb the
ropes in the gym were taunted until they wished they'd never
been born.

Sophie was not only too nice to be an Upper East Side
girl. Sophie was also way too pretty to be an Upper East Side
girl. I was not. I may have been a dork, but I knew how to
fight back (as in this essay, perhaps). Also, I kind of liked
being a dork: I knew it was material, I knew it was toughen-
ing me up for getting pummeled by *The New York Times Book
Review.*

A few days after Sophie arrived at school, Mom told me
I'd be accompanying Sophie to school in the mornings. I was
gleeful. Mom said she had known Sophie's Mom, Tessa or
something, before, and since Sophie also had a nanny (or two,

who didn't?), the nannies would switch off taking us to school. Mom was happy to see me happy. Mom had just married the divorce lawyer, and the divorce lawyer and I were butting heads on all the issues. Besides which we'd just moved into the huge white co-op in the East Sixties. I was not adjusting to this change well. My endless twice-weekly sessions with the super child shrink Doctor L weren't making me normal (or more importantly, thin).

Oddly, Mom always insisted I be taken to school by someone, usually my nanny or, for that brief, wonderful time in seventh grade, Sophie's nanny. This nanny escort situation didn't end until I was sixteen.

But once Sophie and I started going to school together, school was no longer a drag; in fact it was a pleasure. After school I'd often go over to Sophie's house, which was filled with dried flowers, British cookies, chanting Indian monks, incense, and famous people. Sophie's house was like a dream. Sophie had two younger siblings, Luke and Clover. Luke and Clover were children plucked right out of central casting. Both had Waugh-ish accents, both wore little pastel outfits with ducks on them, and both constantly begged "Mummy" for cookies and presents (in that respect, if no other, they resembled me).

Sophie also had two cats, two dogs, various fish, some turtles, and of course two spiritual advisers (notice all the similarities to Noah's ark?). Sophie's mom, Tessa, wrote children's books and the occasional autobiographical novel. Tessa would lie around in her huge iron king-size bed. She was lanky and thin. She had that perfect white, flawless skin.

People would come and visit Tessa in bed. Tessa was pretty much always in bed. When Tessa wasn't in bed she was at the Plaza or the Pierre or some other hotel "writing."

My mom was a writer, but she didn't write in hotels. She wrote in her sweatpants. My mom wasn't lanky and thin (we're Jewish). My mom didn't have perfect white skin. People didn't visit my mom in bed. My mom fought broken blood vessels like they were PLO suicide bombers. My mom wore glasses. My mom was always on a diet. My mom did, though, have perfect teeth.

It was 1990, I was in seventh grade, and life was perfect. The gymnastics girls quelled their taunting because I now had a friend. And not just any friend, a rare, beautiful, British friend with magnificent handwriting. A different sort of animal, one who wrote thank-you cards, who wore perfume, who kept a journal of all her Technicolor dreams. This girl, this amazing creature, this specimen of perfection (except for her violently yellow, scraggly teeth—she was of course British) intrigued the entire class. Sophie intimidated most of the other kids; they stayed away, thus leaving us to sit in her amazing town house, eat cookies, and talk.

Sophie and I talked a lot. Mostly she talked and I ate. Sometimes we'd sit with her mother while her mother lay in bed and occasionally added a sarcastic quip. Sophie was alarmingly brilliant. Her stories were fascinating. Sophie would tell me about all the other places she had lived, all the other schools she had gone to, all the other friends she had had. Even though we were in the seventh grade, Sophie had already been to ten or eleven schools. Sophie told me about all the boys she'd been in love with. She told me about her many trips to India. She explained that you can't drink the water in India because it gives you diarrhea, a fact I found to be one of the most amusing things I had ever heard. "Not only can you not drink the water but you can't eat ice, or ice cream, or even fruit cleaned in the water. If you do then you get diarrhea." Maybe it's just because I think the word *diarrhea* is inherently funny.

Sophie told me about all the houses she'd lived in. Sophie's accent was captivating. Her sense of humor was hilarious. She had a dark, witty, and brooding personality, like the bastard child of Dorothy Parker and Graydon Carter.

Life seemed precarious even then, even on the very iso-lated Upper East Side. America was seconds from invading Kuwait, Milli Vanilli was just about to get stripped of their Grammy Award for "Girl You Know It's True," and the Cold War was just about to officially end.

And then all of a sudden (a few months into the school year) the other kids wanted to be friends with Sophie. This distressed me. Celia wanted to be friends with Sophie. Steph-anie and Elizabeth slept over at Sophie's house. The gymnas-tics girls made overtures toward Sophie. Fred, Connor, and Justin all wanted to go out with Sophie. Even in the tiny Day School, where there are only thirty kids in a class, Sophie was getting popular. And with popularity came busyness. Sophie didn't have time to go buy ugly plaid shirts at the local over-priced boutique-slash-drug-front. Sophie didn't have time to go to the Candle Cafe with me. And Sophie, being the benevolent quintessence of all that is good, didn't drop me.

But I felt jealous, worried, concerned. I had known since the appearance of my stepfather (the lovely divorce lawyer, husband number 4) that sharing wasn't "fun." No matter what the goodly Doctor L said, I knew more parents didn't necessarily equal more attention (especially if those parents went on a monthlong honeymoon and only brought me back some flip-flops).

Sophie made time for me, and seventh grade went on. I got more pimples. I got fatter. I got strep throat like six times that year. Sophie got her period for the first time. Tessa and Mom took us out for tea at a fancy hotel to celebrate. I was mortified. Good-humored Sophie thought it was wildly amusing. It was during my agita over that outing (and about periods in general) that I realized Sophie was just one of those people who enjoyed life, unlike me and the rest of the Jews. Six thousand years in the desert seem to have left some scars.

Tessa took us to this weird spa where we were wrapped in seaweed and then left in a room for a long time. Mom and Ken took us to see *Cyrano de Bergerac,* starring Gérard Depardieu. We went out for Indian food during the great blizzard of '93. Life was fun. I was Jappy. She was British. Things were great: Nelson Mandela was freed from jail after over twenty-seven years, the lambada became the forbidden dance, and Earth Day happened. Then all of a sudden one day, it was June, and school was almost over.

In late May, Celia and some of the gymnastics girls came over to Sophie's large limestone town house for a sleepover. I wasn't there, but it wasn't an unfamiliar scene. A disagreement happened, a conflict about what movie to watch, and the gymnastics girls got annoyed with how perfect and proper Sophie was, so they took all of the food in Sophie's fridge and left it out on the counter to go bad. Sophie was (as usual) nice about it. So the girls upped the ante. They threw things, ruined some art (nothing major), they tortured her pets (a move common to private school girls on the Upper East Side and Colombian drug lords). But Sophie was again tragically nice. So some of the other gymnastics girls spat on Sophie's face. Then Sophie cried, and all the girls left her alone in her big rented town house off Park Avenue, with her rotting food and her traumatized pets.

So it was with the knowledge that Sophie was way too nice for the Upper East Side that we graduated seventh grade. We all left for the summer; that's what city kids do. They flee the melting asphalt for the bugs, skinned knees, and dirt of the suburbs. The gymnastics girls went to gymnastics camp. The musical kids went to music camp. Celia went to some other summer camp where she could torture other people besides me. I went to a particularly awful socialist summer camp called Buck's Rock that my mother was forced to go to and that I will force my children to go to because I am a bad, spiteful, malicious person.

When I came back from camp, someone else had moved into the enormous limestone town house on Seventy-first Street and Park Avenue. Tessa Dahl had taken Sophie, Luke, Clover, and the nannies and the dogs and the cats and the iron bed covered in iron roses to go live in an ashram, which turned out to be a sham. Tessa, Sophie, Clover, Luke, and the nannies and the dogs and the cats ended up having to leave the ashram in the middle of the night with whatever they could carry. They moved to London.

Eighth grade started. Elizabeth and Stephanie reluctantly became my friends, but their hearts really weren't in it. Celia continued to torture me, but she was also busy applying to prep schools. We were all frantically applying to high schools. Even the gymnastics girls were too busy with their mind-numbingly phony personal application essays to taunt me. The Day School ended in eighth grade back then, and we were totally brainwashed about how we needed to get into a "good" high school so that we could get into an Ivy. Of course none of us went to Ivy League schools (most of us were busy in jail at that point), except Celia, who went to Yale with such intellectual luminaries as Claire Danes.

I heard Sophie went to boarding school back in England. I was miserable without her. I got into a high school where everyone was skinny, beautiful, and mean (and stupid—just kidding. Okay I'm not. Yes I am. No I'm not).

I started ninth grade. I walked past Sophie's town house all the time. I missed her so much. I heard Sophie and Tessa moved to the countryside. I dreamed of Sophie almost every night. I talked about her incessantly to Doctor L. I dreamed about her beautiful house, all her perfect things: the dried flowers, the iron bed, the checked floors, the ceiling of pressed leather showing all the signs of the zodiac, her clothing, the smell of her perfume, the color of the thank-you cards she used, the pages of her journal, and the curve of her letters.

Life changed, and I finally (not a moment too soon) hit adolescence. Doctor L convinced me to start losing weight. I was at that point a big, fat fat ass, a female, adolescent Michael Moore (about two hundred pounds and five six or five seven). I stopped eating ten doughnuts a day. I trimmed it back to five doughnuts a day and I started losing weight. I think that taking huge, heaping handfuls of diet pills might have also helped. I love diet pills. Also, I started smoking two packs of Marlboro cigarettes a day. Can I just say that I love cigarettes? I love cigarettes so much. I love smoking. I love smoke. I love walking behind a smoker. I love getting a face full of someone's exhale. I love lighting that first cigarette. I love the head rush. I even love the green phlegm. Where was I?

I still walked down Seventy-first Street every chance I got, except now I ran down Seventy-first Street 'cause I was wired on diet pills and smoking a cigarette and hallucinating because I had not had solid food since I could remember. I still looked for Sophie everywhere. And sometimes even saw her, though usually she also had three heads and was on a tricycle with a little white dog named Larry.

Then in the summer before eleventh grade, I went with Mom on her book tour to London and I saw Sophie. She waited for me downstairs in the hotel bar. I was Humbert Humbert (except thin, insane, on diet pills, Jewish, and a girl), and she was Lolita (except she was older than I was, she was bigger than I was, and she was British). She looked old. We drank vodka gimlets. We smoked. She was seventeen. I was sixteen. We were a couple of old broads. She was heavy. She told me she was going to go to secretarial school. She told me she was in love with a certain hideous, untalented, slightly demonic painter who had also made a play for me earlier in the summer but whom I hadn't liked because he didn't have any cocaine (though he had sworn up and down to me that he had a plethora of drugs). She ate the nuts out of the dish on the table in the lobby. I wouldn't have eaten those nuts because I looked at that bowl and thought, Hello, hepatitis! I felt bad for her (especially now that I was sure she was gonna get hepatitis). But I also felt happy because I was doing better than she was.

I stopped dreaming about Sophie because she was just like me now. I stopped wondering about Sophie because now I knew. The Sophie myth sort of died in my eyes. I looked back on those days in seventh grade and realized that Sophie's mom wasn't in New York for the culture. She was in New York because Brian De Palma (director of such mediocrities as *The Bonfire of the Vanities* and *Snake Eyes*) had just broken her heart. I realized that Tessa wasn't in hotels so that she could write. She went to hotels to have an affair with a certain actor. I finally figured out that Sophie had been the product of a romance between a nineteen-year-old Tessa and a recently divorced Julian Holloway. Sophie had, when we were in seventh grade, shown me a picture of the two gorgeous, tan, lanky Brits swimming in a pool in the South of France. She mentioned later that her dad was filming *Sammy's Super T-Shirt*.

I realized all sorts of other things too. I realized that Sophie was profoundly sad, and that her childhood was very difficult. More importantly, I realized I was a jealous, catty bitch who was shallow, shallow, shallow. The Dahls weren't happy, they were just really rich and really good looking and really British. Though isn't that really what happiness is—

a warm trust fund, no body fat, and a tolerance for coronation chicken?

Sophie came again to New York City in the summer. She stayed with her grandma. She got her teeth capped, as I had done a few months before. Teeth capping was kind of like the New York equivalent to the great Los Angeles tradition of the sweet sixteen boob job. She was in love with some other boy. She was bigger then. We sweated together on the city streets. Her breasts reached maximum proportion. They became distracting. I turned seventeen. She turned eighteen. We drank frappacinos.

Two years passed; I dropped out of three colleges. I ended up at Hazelden, which I loved. I love, love, love rehab. It is also the thing I am best at. I gained thirty pounds in rehab, but I did get off diet pills, cocaine, Valium, and vodka. I came home from rehab. Sophie called me. I told her I couldn't see her. I really didn't want to see her because I felt like such a loser for moving back into my parents' house again, and for dropping out of college and for incurring an enormous amount of debt.

So I didn't see Sophie, a move I really, really regretted afterward. I started to abstain from drugs and alcohol. It took me a few years to really get clean. I didn't slip, but emotional abstinence was harder to achieve than physical abstinence. It took me a year to stop calling people like Toby Young, author of *How to Lose Friends and Alienate People* (whom I didn't know but called because I was nuts). I was very depressed as I started to get clean.

I started to see Sophie on the covers of magazines (*Tatler,*

Italian *Vogue,* British *Vogue*). Sophie got thinner and thinner, though at the same time she also got larger and larger. One day I looked up and there she was looking down on me. Giant Sophie, clad in a red raincoat, smiling, holding a duck, extolling the virtues of Banana Republic rain gear. I looked up at her. She looked down at me. I looked up at the duck. The duck looked down at me. I wondered if I stepped in front of that speeding car whether it would stop or whether it would hit me.

The Sophie myth was back! Only now she wasn't some anonymous little blond British girl, she no longer belonged to me. She belonged to the world. There were now websites devoted to her. There were now posters of her for sale on the Internet. Sophie had quickly become a fixture on Page Six. All of a sudden Sophie was more famous than her mom, or my mom, or anyone that I had ever known. All of a sudden Sophie was dating Mick Jagger. And it had all happened before my very eyes. First she had been a "plus size" model (though she was just sort of the size of a normal person), then she had gotten thin, thin, thin and turned into a supermodel.

It occurred to me at that moment that Sophie was huge, a giant really, and that I was just five feet, eight inches tall (very tall for a descendant of squat Jewish herring merchants). I realized at that moment it was a great tragedy that I hadn't become a supermodel too. In the end, I wonder, if there is a God, then why aren't we all supermodels? Why can't we all be featured on Page Six? Why can't we all be huge, naked, and British? And if not the first two, why can't we all just have beautiful accents? Is that too much to ask? Is it? *Is it?*

what's in joan collins's box?

✳

MY LIFE BEGAN when I met Joan Collins. Before that the world was a dark, barren place filled only with Moon Pies (vanilla, chocolate, and orange flavor), circus peanuts, marshmallow Peeps, caramel Tastykakes, Jelly Belly jelly beans, and grade school. I was thirteen when my mom brought me to London for spring break. She was hoping that by getting away from American food I might win the battle of the bulge. While in London I ate many, many, many things. Some of the things I ate in London were Flake chocolate, Smarties, and coronation chicken.

Then one day, as I was shoveling something into my mouth, Mom told me she had a surprise for me. I was going to meet the great Joan Collins. Now, I wasn't some hick from Connecticut (well, technically, I was). I grew up in the center of the Western world. I "knew" (or had met) many celebrities—Susan Dey's daughter, Marisa Berenson's daughter, Faye

Dunaway's son, Roald Dahl's granddaughter, Andrea Dworkin, and Dr. Ruth.

Mom dressed me in my best peach-colored sweatshirt decorated with kittens sketched in pink, puffy paint, and rolled me out to meet Joan Collins. We were twenty minutes late, because I was busy eating clotted cream, which I liked a lot, although I found its resemblance to cottage cheese (a Weight Watchers diet staple) somewhat unsettling. Joan was thirty minutes late. If Joan had been more famous (say as famous as Miss Jennifer Lopez), she would have been later. This brings us to celebrity rule number 1: the more famous the celebrity, the later the arrival.

The restaurant we met in was called San Lorenzo. Lots of celebrities hang out at San Lorenzo. Some celebrities like San Lorenzo because of its mediocre food, and others like it because of the photographers who wait outside, but most like it because other celebrities go there. This relates to celebrity rule number 2: as Babs says, "People who need people are the luckiest people in the world." This is especially true for celebrities. You see, it's very, very hard to be famous. Just because they're rich, just because they ride around in private jets, just because they can buy anything they want, just because they never have to worry about money, doesn't mean that when you cut them they don't bleed.

Joan drank flat water (Joan tells us in her great manifesto *Joan's Way* that "fizzy water causes wrinkles") and ate small bits of boiled fish. Mom had a salad. I had French fries, fried fish, pasta, a whole loaf of bread, three Cokes, and two desserts. I wasn't fat but chubby, chubby enough to injure horses and to have to wear riding jackets that were sized "husky"

(Isn't that sad? Don't you feel so bad for me? Don't you just want to hug me? Well, why not take that love for me and go buy a couple hundred copies of my book; don't forget, five books will help me ease the pain of my tragic, tragic childhood, ten books will make the pain dissipate, and two hundred books will cure me of the emotional polio I suffer from).

We sat at a coveted corner table. Mom sat across from Joan. Since it was the early nineties, both women still had Nancy Reagan hair, shoulder pads, and clothing made of flammable fabric. Mom even wore a jacket decorated in rhinestones.

I knew Joan was famous because people stared at her like she was the Elephant Man. Mom and I pretended not to notice everyone else in the restaurant staring at Joan's every sip of flat water, but the sad truth was Joan's voluptuous hair cast an enormous shadow over all of us. Our winning personalities and good teeth were no match for fame, the Ebola virus of high society (except without the blood, or the death, or the tragedy but otherwise, yes, fame is just like Ebola, except that Ebola happens to poor people in rural Africa, and fame happens to, bafflingly enough, the Baldwin brothers).

It was a rainy day in London, the Cold War had just ended, and the conversation shifted to yachts. I'd never been on a yacht. Sure, I'd been on the Circle Line (a touristy boat that trudges through the toxic waste in the East River), and I'd been on a cruise ship—where else does one meet Dr. Ruth?—but I'd never been on a yacht. This turned out to be a lucky thing, as I later found that almost every traveling activity makes me violently motion sick. Joan was holding forth about her famous friends. As I mentioned before, famous people need other famous people for support because being famous is so incredibly difficult.

Joan started talking about Valentino. She regaled us with stories of the wonderful times she had had on Valentino's yacht. It was clear to me that Valentino was extraordinarily supportive and sensitive. I found it heartwarming to consider the generosity that must have inspired him to invite onto his yacht (for days at a time, it seemed) the tanned young things I was hearing about. Fashion designers are known for their sensitivity, for their love of women, puppies, and orphans. I assumed the nubile young things were homeless. Most fashion designers are actually former Peace Corps volunteers or missionaries. Between bites of pasta and French fries, I told Joan Collins that I too would like to go on Valentino's yacht.

"Moooooom, Mom, Mom, MOM, Mom!"

"Yes, darling," Mom said, looking away from Joan Collins's enormous head of hair.

"Mooooom!" I said as I knocked over a small silver bowl filled with catsup. Catsup oozed across the table; slow, thick, it seemed to be heading toward Joan's enormous shoulder pads. A despondent-looking busboy ran over and scooped up the offending catsup in his napkin.

"Darling, Joan is trying to say something, let Mommy have a minute."

The chandelier sparkled and was reflected in the shining tile. Across the room two models smoked cigarettes and drank white wine out of huge goblets. "You must come with me, darling! You'd love Valentino's yacht so much." Joan Collins stabbed her fork into her salad.

"MMMMMMMMMMom, MMMMMMMom, I wanna go on Valentino's yacht. I bet Valentino has fish and chips on his yacht. Ohh, and Swedish fish."

"I wouldn't bank on it," interjected Mom as she took another sip of flat water.

"I wannnna go on Valentino's yacht," I pleaded again over the din of glasses clinking and waiters spilling things.

"Ohh, no, not as you are now, why you're too fat to go on Valentino's yacht," Joan Collins quipped.

For two long seconds the world stopped. There was silence. It was like the Kennedy assassination, combined with Napoleon heading for Elba to create pastry, with a smattering of bombs raining on London during the Blitz, and a touch of Pearl Harbor, plus a tiny bit of the advent of the Wonderbra— all this impact made the silence deafening.

What had happened here? What egregious crime had been committed? I knew. Mom knew. Joan Collins knew. Joan Collins had called me fat. It was at that very moment that I knew the world must hear my story, my hardship, my tragedy.

Even at the tender age of thirteen, I knew that I'd be dining out on this faux pas for the next decade. Mom looked at Joan in horror. Even then, at the tender age of forty-seven, Mom knew she'd be paying for the therapy to help me through this faux pas for at least the next decade. Joan looked at the tiled floor. Even at the tender age of two thousand years old, Joan should have known that loud, obese thirteen-year-olds turn into very menacing twenty-four-year-olds with book contracts and Apple laptops.

Joan backpedaled. "Of course I'm too fat for Valentino's yacht, too. I mean, we all are. Erica's too fat, too."

But it was too late. Even at thirteen I knew there would be a time when the people at *People* magazine would need to hear this story. Even at thirteen I knew that this was going to be my truth, that this was going to be one of the defining moments in my life.

Remorse is an odd thing. Napoleon did not feel remorse for burning Moscow, but Joan is much taller than Napoleon. Joan felt bad. Joan felt so bad that from that moment on Joan was unbelievably, alarmingly, disturbingly nice to me. Alexis Carrington loved me.

We finished lunch. Mom took me back to the hotel, and the week ended with little more excitement, except for the sampling of profiteroles (yum) and Cadbury Crisp. We flew home on a Pan Am airplane that had two floors. I went back to grade school. Mom went back to writing. Hong Kong went back to China. OJ went back to court. People started having cybersex. OJ didn't go to jail. The Dow hit four thousand, then a year later five thousand. Jerry Garcia died. OJ still didn't go to jail. Two years passed, I went to high school, and Joan Collins apparently still felt bad about calling me fat.

This, coupled with the fact that her daughter needed a friend to go to Paris with, ended me up as Joan's houseguest for a week. It was a perfect plan; I would stay with Joan for a week before going on to a summer study abroad program with Joan's daughter Katy. Joan would rescue me from the dirt and poverty of the Upper East Side, she would take me away from all that, to see *Riverdance* (two hours of mind-numbing foot-tapping "entertainment"). Joan Collins would be my Fresh Air Fund host. But let us ask why Joan Collins would let me stay in her house.

Joan Collins is not rich. She doesn't get money every time *Dynasty* airs in China, India, Italy, France, or Denmark. She doesn't get residuals at all. Joan Collins has to work to earn a living. She always has. One must wonder if there was some supremely self-destructive force that guided her into four failed marriages, a contract where she didn't get residuals, and agreeing to have a certain little fat kid stay with her for a week in July.

Normally, I would now go into a seemingly endless rant about Joan's daughter, but I won't because Katy is very sweet, polite, lovely, charming, and adorable. And I feel camaraderie with her, due to the fact that Katy is, like me (Jon Fast and Erica Jong were married from 1978 to 1981) the product of a third marriage (Ron Kass and Joan were married from 1972 to 1983). And while I'm being sensitive, let me just add that Joan is a really good mom to Katy and loves her a lot.

Joan has other children, but they're much older. They are both from marriage number 2, to Anthony Newley, which lasted from 1963 to 1970, and for some reason I just have this feeling in my bones that if I write about them I will regret it.

So at age fifteen Mackenzie Phillips was having sex with Mick Jagger, and I was lugging my suitcase to a certain house on Eaton Place. Eaton Place is a very ritzy street in London that consists of two rows of large, identical white limestone town houses (think Levittown for the rich). Joan lived in an apartment in one of those identical limestone buildings. I rang the buzzer. Joan greeted me.

Joan Collins is a goddess; actually, that's not true, she is

God, the God, the big one from Rome. Here's how I know that Joan Collins is God—she has the gift of eternal life. She looks abnormally young, almost like she's had plastic surgery, yet we know she hasn't had plastic surgery because she writes in *Joan's Way* that all she does to keep her face tight as a snare drum is avoid fizzy water.

For the doubters I've included a description of *Joan's Way* from her website; I think it proves my theory that she's God: How does Joan Collins manage to look so groomed and glamorous all the time? Well, *Joan's Way* is her fantastic tips on how to look amazing, be sexy and have loads of energy throughout your life. Distilled from a lifetime in the limelight, Joan brings the inside knowledge of Hollywood glamour together with commonsense guidelines on diet, exercise and well-being. Joan lifts the secrets of super youth, showing how to slow down the aging process, through exercise and eating right for life.

Also a few words on Joan's philosophy of life, further proof that she is our savior: "William White epitomizes in these few words how I have tried to live my life. My life has changed radically since I started *Dynasty*. The stardom that I never tried to attain as a young actress I have now. How long will it last—who knows? This is the toughest of professions. Very tough. Flavour of the month changes rapidly. Only the strongest, the cleverest and the most resilient survive—but survival is not the only objective" (www.joancollins.net). From this abstract we can see so much about Joan Collins, the woman. We can also see an example of celebrity rule number 11: the importance of fame seeming accidental, as if you never wanted to be famous ("The stardom that I never tried to attain as a young actress I have now"). Now, I don't know a lot (I have six credits from five years of college), but I know one thing, which is that people don't get famous by accident (they get famous on *Survivor*).

But there's more meaning than just the enactment of celebrity rule number 11 in this excerpt from Joan's website. A larger than life question has been asked. "But survival is not the only objective." What is the other objective?

Joan Collins came to the door wearing a turban. For a minute I was sure I'd mistakenly arrived at the home of Alexis Carrington. Joan Collins looked amazing. Her skin was flawless. Her eyes the most piercing blue. Her robe made of the finest silk. Her shoulder pads crafted of the finest polyester. Spilling out of her mouth were words in that elegant pseudo-British accent: "Dahllling, it's so wonderful to see you. Yes, so wonderful. Why, you've lost weight, haven't you?"

And yet something was wrong with the way Joan Collins looked. Yes, the star of *Dynasty*, *The Bitch*, and *The Stud*, and the author of such notable books as *Joan's Way*, *Star Quality*, *Prime Time*, *Second Act*, *Too Damn Famous*, *Past Imperfect*, *My Secrets*, *My Friends' Secrets*, and *The Joan Collins Beauty Book* had the most dramatically tweezed eyebrows I had ever almost not seen. The essence of Joan Collins's eyebrows had gone the way of the Berlin Wall.

Please don't think from what I've said that I don't love Joan. Because I do love Joan Collins. And hers is the best-case scenario for any young actress. At the danger of sounding like her publicist, let me say Joan Collins has miraculously maintained her dignity (and I think her beauty) through *Dynasty*, *Playboy*, and the authoring of a novel called *Too Damn Fa-*

mous. But also I love Joan Collins 'cause she is a grand dame, tough as an alligator handbag but still supporting large numbers of family members including several ex-husbands.

As Joan pressed me to her bony breast, I knew that I loved her and would have to turn on her, just as all writers must give everything away, must turn on their families, their characters, their subjects, their parents, their third-grade teachers, their stylists, their beloved three-legged dog Tripod, and ultimately themselves. "Alas, these pencils, too, have been distributed among the characters in my books to keep fiction's children busy; they are not quite my own now" (*Speak, Memory,* p. 101).

I knew I was going to have to make use of this experience, much in the way I made use of my experience at rehab, my experiences with drugs, my experiences with eating disorders, and pretty much everything else that's ever happened to me. I am, after all, my material.

Joan led me up a few steps out of the little entrance hall and into her sprawling two-bedroom apartment. Joan's bedroom was in the front of the house, and the guest room (my room) was toward the kitchen. The whole apartment was piled floor to ceiling with antiques. Antiques were everywhere, floor to ceiling, ceiling to floor, in the corners, out of the corners, in the closets (they weren't the only things in the closets), against the walls everywhere. The most popular antique in Joan's world was the sideboard. Joan Collins had three sideboards. In the guest room there was a small bed, an enormous sideboard, many cabinets, many little antique tables, and tons of art. Needless to say, I bruised both my baby toes on her cornucopia of cabinetry.

Tchotchkelehs were everywhere too. Little knickknacks, battery boxes, figurines, paperweights, and other little things one would be able to scoop up on the Home Shopping Network if the Home Shopping Network sold Limoges.

But I had no time to think about decor; I was hungry after my long flight. In those two hours since touchdown, I'd consumed only two éclairs, a large muffin, an almond Danish, and a chocolate bar. So I went into Joan's kitchen to fix myself a five-course meal. Unfortunately, I was about to learn celebrity rule number 3: celebrities don't eat. Barring a special occasion or an eating scene, celebrities don't eat. And Joan didn't disprove celebrity rule number 3. In Joan Collins's kitchen I found—bran chips cereal, bran biscuits, skim milk, and Marks & Spencer's coronation chicken.

I am not saying Joan Collins is not a good hostess. She is an amazing hostess. She got me a guest pass to her gym for the week I was staying with her. So every morning that I stayed with Joan Collins, I would get up and go to the gym. Maybe Joan was helping me get in shape for Valentino's yacht.

Now, the gym was all the way across London off the Kings Road. Sometimes I'd walk to Joan's gym and sometimes I'd take a taxi and sometimes Joan's driver would drive me there. One morning I woke blurry-eyed to the smell of fresh coffee. Joan offered her driver to drive me to her gym. I agreed. She requested only one thing.

"Molly, darling. I was hoping that you'd let Paul drive you to the gym," Joan said as we were drinking coffee in her kitchen. She wore yet another silk robe, thus evoking celebrity rule number 4: celebrities try to wear robes and pajamas as much as humanly possible. Joan wore the turban (a usual sight at this point). Joan's boyfriend at the time, the thirty-eight-year-old Adonis Robin Hurlstone (too easy a target), was lurking around, too.

Joan's houseman had bought a pound of doughnuts, and I was scarfing them down. "Joan, baby, anything. You know I'm your go-to girl on all that stuff. I got you covered, babe." Actually I really just muttered a nervous "Sure."

"Darling, you see, I was hoping you could drop off this box with this, um, friend of mine. Would that be okay, darling? Would you mind that, darling?" How could I say no? How could I do anything but what Ms. Alexis Carrington asked? But deep down I knew that taking this box was a mistake. I knew that this story would end badly. Besides, I thought for a minute. Was I Kato Kaelin? Was this what my young life had come to? Was I just some girl running errands for the rich and famous in return for free room, board, pounds of doughnuts, bran flakes, and gym membership? Yes! Yes, I was a fat, Jewish Kato Kaelin.

So I took the box. The box was a small, square, white cake box, maybe twelve inches by twelve inches. It was tied in red bakery string. The sides of this cake box were taped. Joan Collins never expressly told me not to look in the box. She never said, "Don't look in the box."

Of course the sides were taped, the string was tied tightly, and I was, even at the tender age of fifteen, genteel enough to know not to open a box that was taped together, and yet . . .

I got in the black town car. I sat in the backseat. The car smelled new and plasticky. Paul turned on some classical music. I put Joan Collins's box on my lap. It was yet another rainy day in London. I was chewing on some Polo mints. I was averaging four rolls of Polo mints a day. My Polo mint addiction was offsetting my smoking. I thought about Joan's box. I felt bad because even then I knew I was a writer. I knew I'd have to write about all of this, and yet I did like Joan and Katy. I liked everyone, but I liked making good-natured fun of them, too. Making fun of people was in my Polish vaudeville, smoked whitefish merchant blood. I was torn.

This might have been a different story if I hadn't opened Joan Collins's box. This might have been a story of longing, a story of secrets, of forgiveness, of family values, of small-town living and what's really important. This might have been *The Bridges of Upper East Side County*.

But I didn't find love in Joan Collins's box. I didn't find what was really important or the spirit of Christmas. I found a wig in Joan Collins's box, and that's when I realized that Joan Collins was not all she's cracked up to be. In a more profound sense, I realized when I opened Joan Collins's box that Joan Collins was actually just a normal person, just like you or me, if we were famous with bad hair, and married to a man almost one hundred years younger. See, when I opened Joan Collins's box, that day, in the mid-nineties, in London, I realized something: I realized that celebrities are just like us, if we were famous.

venice

*

"VENICE IS SINKING," Mom said. She was looking in the mirror. Fully clothed, I was sitting on the side of the empty bathtub.

"Then I don't really want to go there," I said and then burst into tears. I was seven.

"Well, it's sinking very slowly."

"I still don't ever want to go there." I had red hair and was adorable in the way that seven-year-olds are.

"Well, we have to go there. We've rented an apartment there."

"Why? What if it sinks when we're there?"

"It won't."

"I think it will, and then we'll die," I said, and then ran off crying to my nanny Margaret, who explained to me that Venice wasn't sinking at all. The truth was, of course, that they were both wrong: Venice had sunk long ago.

As a girl I went to Venice with lovers, husbands, and men with wives. They were all potential stepfathers to me. As a girl I saw love affairs going sour, children getting ruined, and smart Venetians living off the fat of the land. Ultimately, everything I ever needed to know about life, I learned from a place where no one pays taxes, no one ever scoops the poop, and the idea of not smoking in a restaurant is laughable.

Margaret came to Venice the first time with a Stew Leonard's shopping bag. She knew that if she got a photo of herself holding the bag, the photo would be prominently displayed on the "Stew's bags around the world" wall, and she would also get a free frozen yogurt or ice cream, which of course she would immediately give to me. Stew Leonard's was more to us than just a large grocery store in Norwalk, Connecticut, owned by some guy who didn't pay taxes. Stew's was a religion. Margaret and I loved Stew's. We'd get up at seven on a Saturday, jump into Margaret's Geo Prizm, and drive up the Post Road. We'd then wait approximately fifteen minutes for a parking space. Then we'd jump out of the Prizm and head into the earthly paradise with a supersize shopping cart.

"Honey, you can have a yogurt after we're done shopping, okay?"

I'd smile with the knowledge there were tons of tasters of cookies and cakes floating around Stew's. "Okay!"

Then we'd go nuts. First Margaret would take me to the petting zoo, where stinky goats and ugly chickens flirted with each other, where flies buzzed happily around the heads of confused looking cows. Then we'd hit the animatronic dancing cows/bears/dogs, all with banjos, all singing "Oh Susanna." Then and only then would we start shopping: first we'd hit the baked goods, then the milk, the prepared foods, the meats, the fishes, and let's not forget the loaves. Yes, as regularly as Margaret and I went to church (every Sunday), we'd go to Stew's. And sometimes Stew's was more spiritual than church (imagine my shock at finding out that I was Jewish).

And all of that spirituality would end with a strawberry yogurt with colored sprinkles.

In Venice we set off at once to find the perfect spot for Margaret to pose with the bag. A spot that screamed both "Venice!" and "I'm standing here with a shopping bag to get a free ice cream cone." We had a mission—a mission we accomplished in the first three hours of our first day. Margaret perched high on the Accademia bridge, smiling, with a Stew Leonard's bag in hand. I stood on the fondamenta and took the fateful picture that would win us our free ice cream and hang on Stew's wall of photos. That left only twenty-nine days and twenty-one hours of unair-conditioned Venetian summer to kill.

Mom had rented an apartment on Giudecca. It's fair to say that Giudecca is the mustached, double-chinned, elderly aunt of mainland Venice, though its one good quality (besides the fact that it, like the rest of Venice, is sinking) is that it's the island that houses the hotel where the brilliant policy maker, the Gustav Mahler of shopping, former President Ronald Reagan stayed: the famous Cipriani.

Mom would rent the place every summer for the next four years. It was a charming house with almost no air-conditioning, except in Mom's bedroom. Mom's bedroom was an oasis of cool. The rest of the house was unbearably hot, so hot that we would close the shutters and I would lie on the marble

bathroom floor and daydream about being whisked away, res-
cued by the heir to the Frederick air conditioner fortune.

The apartment was the second floor of a rotting sixteenth-
century palazzo. It was filled with dusty, splintery furniture. I
slept in an ancient canopy bed that would release a great
cloud of dust every time I'd get in it. The comforter on this
ancient bed was so old that it tore when I pulled it up to
cover my eyes as I listened to the noise of rats tunneling inside
the walls and underneath the wall-to-wall carpeting. In the
morning I would wake, covered in dust, to find more rat tunnels in the carpet.

The only cool place in my universe (besides my mother's
air-conditioned bedroom) was the Cipriani Hotel pool, a
pool that had been made almost twice its intended size by accident when someone on a phone call confused meters with
feet. Mom was allowed to swim in the Cipriani pool because
of her celebrity status. Margaret and I were allowed to join
her because we were related to Erica Jong. The Cipriani
Hotel was where I learned about how the other half lives.

In Piazza San Marco fat tourists feed fat pigeons. They
look in their guidebooks; they take pictures of each other in
front of giant stone lions. They speak German or English or
Japanese to each other. They eat overpriced ice cream. They
ride in gondolas and follow people with umbrellas around.
They look at their maps. They sweat. They buy T-shirts of
kittens dressed up as gondolieri.

But just a short boat ride away, across the Giudecca canal,
there is a place where a chicken sandwich costs forty dollars
and Stephanie Seymour dances around in a white bathing
suit. This place, this unearthly paradise, is the Cipriani Hotel.

And through its manicured gardens one can spot the great and the near great and the merely very rich, as well as their entourages.

I always swam at the Cipriani Hotel pool, but I never stayed there, not once. This was because the rooms in the Cipriani Hotel are at least a thousand dollars a night, and the good rooms are much, much more than that. The Cipriani Hotel was the kind of place you stayed in when Paramount Pictures was paying the tab.

Margaret and I would go swim at the Cipriani Hotel almost every day. We came from our roasting, rotting house to this paradise. We would enter off of Giudecca. To get into the hotel we would walk though the servants' quarters, past empty beer bottles, laundry hung on lines to dry, and stray cats in compromising positions. The main entrance to the hotel was of course by boat. The servants' entrance wasn't supposed to be used; it was supposed to dissuade you from going out to Giudecca, to the few small, poor shops on the underpopulated island or to the Harry's Dolce (Harry's Dolce is the poor, six-fingered cousin to the famous Harry's Bar) on the other side of the island.

It was at the Cipriani pool that I met two of the most important people in my childhood. Sure, there were people who figured much larger in my life—nannies, shrinks, pets, parents—but it was these two children that made me understand the seriousness of my situation. I did not meet these young luminaries during my first or second stay in Venice. I met them on my third stay in the haunted palazzo, when I was an awkward thirteen years old.

Luke (please note that I am not using this character's real

name; instead, I am calling him Luke because of his uncanny resemblance to Luke Skywalker or something) came to Venice with his Irish nanny and stayed in a poolside suite at the Cipriani. Luke's nanny and Margaret immediately became best friends. Margaret was Scottish, but she liked the Irish anyway.

Luke's mother was a famous actress. Most likely Luke has never been described without the use of the name of his famous mother, and that is why I won't mention her once. This is not to say I think myself better than any shameless name-dropper who came before me. I am surely no better (though I am filled with less malice) than Julia Phillips or, now that I think about it, Dr. Seuss, who is my personal literary hero (but that is for another day).

And let me just add I drop a lot of names in this book, but they are dropped not just to sell books (though that would be nice) but also for the greater good of mankind.

"Hi, I'm Luke! My nanny said I should come and say hi to you. Because you're the only other kid I've seen here in the last three weeks. Are you staying in the hotel? I am. My mom's a famous actress. She's very famous. She's in a big movie. She says this movie will be her comeback. We're staying here all summer. But I live in Los Angeles. Though my dad lives in London. He's a famous photographer, but I only ever see him on Christmas. His name is—"

"That's cool. I'm Molly. My mom writes erotic novels. I think she really writes dirty books. We're renting this gross house that's filled with dirt on the other side of Giudecca. Recently I got heatstroke and barfed four separate times in an hour. Isn't that cool? Do you have any video games?"

"Barfing is cool."

"You know what else is cool," I continued. "There are rats in my bedroom, and they tunnel under the carpet and make rat tunnels. They have a whole rat city in my room."

"Cool, can I come see?"

And so a great friendship was born. Luke had brown freckles. He was profoundly bored. Not to kill the suspense, but let me just say now that Luke's mom's comeback film ended up going straight to video.

Luke and I met there, that day at the huge Cipriani pool. There we discovered that if you drank ten nonalcoholic fruit drinks, you could barf up blue barf. There we discovered that if you taped grapes to your head they stuck and actually made quite a disgusting hat. There we discovered Pignoli Nut. Pignoli Nut didn't have a nanny. She was just left to wander around on her own. She was lanky with long, brown hair. She was beautiful like her mother. She had brown glossy eyes like brown, glossy ice cream. She had skinny legs and perfect, tan arms. She had freckles. She was a nymph who entranced every middle-aged man she came in contact with. I was no Lolita. I didn't entrance every man I came in contact with. In fact, I didn't entrance any man I came in contact with, unless *entrance* means nagging him to buy me ice cream and then stepping on his toes.

Her mother swished Pignoli Nut away when Pignoli Nut came anywhere near her. As self-centered as I was, even I noticed how lonely Pignoli Nut was. I remember meeting her mother, a famous socialite-actress. The mother (who had packed nothing but wrinkle cream and boxes of Valentino

gowns for her trip to Venice) was smoking cigarettes and looking glamorous with her dark-skinned, gray-haired boyfriend.

"Can't you go off with little Molly Jong and find something to do?"

"But you said we'd go shopping today."

"Mommy's busy," the socialite said and smiled at her
gray-haired boyfriend. They lay in lounge chairs by the pool.
The gray-haired boyfriend smiled back. He wore a gold
chain and a small red bikini Speedo—the combination was
mesmerizing.

"But, Mom."

"Enough, go play with little Molly Jong and her nanny,"
the socialite said. She always called me Molly Jong even
though my name was Molly Jong-Fast. The Fast part just
didn't feel famous enough to say.

"But, Mom."

"Now I'm getting angry."

I felt bad for Pignoli Nut.

I'm not sure I ever even met Luke's famous mom. But I
did watch the movies she'd been given by the academy to see,
and I did hang out in her suite and eat all the food from her
minibar. And we did go to the set of that ill-fated movie.
Luke and I were allowed to fence with the giant, heavy fake
swords. Luke and I were given little cakes from the craft service table. Luke and I were treated as we always were, as
adorable though slightly annoying potential memoirists.

One of the large problems with Luke was that he wasn't
particularly spoiled. He was like me, somewhat spoiled but
kicked into shape by the nanny who was actually raising him.

Margaret's favorite thing to say to me was, "Don't be bad, or I'll sell you to the Indians."

Luke's nanny's favorite thing to say to him was, "Don't be a brat or I'll take you over my knee."

Margaret and Luke's nanny were both Catholics. They bonded over this immediately. Margaret loved going to Italy, because to her, Italy was much closer to God, since the pope was in Rome. Margaret took Luke's nanny to Santa Maria della Salute, a large church with a huge white dome, one of the newer buildings in Venice (it was built in the seventeenth century).

Every Sunday, Margaret would go to church. Margaret had been raised as a Presbyterian but had converted to Catholicism when she married her late husband, Bob. In church Margaret would light candles for Bob, for her daughter who died in infancy, for her three sons, for her father, who died of mustard gas poisoning in World War I. In church Margaret lit candles for me, for Luke, for Mom, for all the past and present potential stepfathers—the southern gentleman, Mr. Pig, and the gentle gentile. In church Margaret got on her knees. In church Margaret clutched her rosary beads. In and out of church Margaret's faith never wavered.

It's funny now that I think about it, years later, pregnant, sitting here in a small room back in Venice in a hotel only a five-minute boat ride from my childhood; on our best days we were more like our nannies than our parents.

Luke and I were also happy, incredibly, insanely, gleefully happy. We would spend days driving the boat that the movie studio supplied for his amusement. We would spend days with our amazing nannies, who would buy us gelato and dote on us endlessly. We would spend days swimming at the Cipriani pool, where the world was serviced by waiters in white jackets and a thirty-dollar bowl of berries was only a finger's snap away.

Some days we happily lost the battle of being anything but what we were; those were the days that we were more like our parents than our nannies.

"I never want to go back to school," Luke said, lounging on a lounge chair and eating twenty dollars' worth of vanilla gelato.

"Never!" I agreed.

"Let's be movie stars when we grow up."

"YES," I shouted.

Of course the movie star spent her days working on her comeback.

Pignoli Nut wandered Venice that summer. She didn't have a nanny. She would get lost for a few hours, and no one would notice. I sometimes wondered if she'd just wander off into a canal one day.

My mom felt bad for Pignoli Nut because Pignoli Nut had no nanny. I felt bad for Pignoli Nut because she limited herself to one gelato a day. Margaret felt bad for Pignoli Nut 'cause she was so darn skinny. *Vogue* magazine also felt bad about Pignoli Nut's skinniness (I'll get to that in a minute).

"I will go to Paris after the summer is over. There I will see my dad. Then I'll head back to L.A.," the lanky, fourteen-year-old Pignoli Nut said, all the while lanking around. "Maybe when I get back to L.A., I will become a model. My mom is a model, you know. She is best friends with Valentino. Valentino said I could model for him. I don't know. I'm so conflicted about modeling."

"Ohh look, ice cream. Margaret, can I get ice cream!!! Pllease?"

"Sometimes I think I will become a famous model. Sometimes I think it is my destiny."

"MARGARET, I need ice cream!!!! Pllllllllllllease."

Pignoli Nut glared. "It's not called ice cream. It's called gelato."

"Can I get some? Please, Margaret!! Please!!!! I like the chocolate chip! It's sooooooo good!"

"God, you're so im-mat-ure."

Pignoli Nut and I hung out some, but I was never too enamored with her. I liked her, don't get me wrong, but the funny, chubby Jewish girl can have only so many friends who look like models. I had to draw the line somewhere and start looking for someone with a little body fat.

But the summer was wonderful. Luke almost steered his boat into a fourteenth-century building. If he had, I think he would have been able to cause a small island off of Giudecca to collapse. I got sunstroke two more times that summer. I puked blue two more times. Margaret bought me and Luke lime green yo-yos that glowed in the dark. Eventually the summer ended. Luke went to Rome with his mother to finish shooting. Margaret and I went home to Connecticut and New York City to resume our normal life of shopping at Stew's, visiting various child psychiatrists all over Manhattan, and going to church. My bags were filled with plastic rosary beads; when my grandmother spotted them hanging on the four posts of my bed, she nearly had a nervous breakdown. Pignoli Nut went to Paris to be fabulous. We all left Venice, because eventually everyone who goes on to have a job must leave Venice.

A few years later Pignoli Nut posed for a Christmas *Vogue* shoot. She was so skinny. I was so fat. Life seemed so unjust! Why did my inability to resist ten Hostess cupcakes shut me off from what seemed like a lucrative and enjoyable career? It was then that I realized we inhabit a godless universe, a universe where, moreover, some are able to travel in private planes and others must fly commercial. Pignoli Nut looked like her natural conclusion—tall, brown-haired, thin, like her mother but lonelier. I was jealous, but then it doesn't take much to make me jealous (a movie deal, a good-looking handbag, an ability to parallel park, a good seat at the trendy health food restaurant where I've been going since birth but still can't get a good table). Pignoli Nut didn't become a model, though. She became a social worker and moved to California.

Luke went home to California. Under very suspicious circumstances (involving some degree of abuse from her boss), the nanny quit. Luke was sent to boarding school in New England the next year. He was thirteen. He spent Christmas and all other holidays with his nanny's family in Ireland. Luke also spent summers in Ireland with his nanny's family. A few months ago I was looking in a magazine, and I saw a picture of Luke and his famous mother at a movie premiere. She looked so interested in him. She looked as if she had adored him his entire life. She looked as if she'd changed his diapers. He looked as if he believed that she had changed his diapers. For a second it felt as if maybe his nanny and I were the only people in the entire world who knew the truth. That really annoyed me.

I think it's fair to say that I learned everything I needed to know from Venice, from a city filled with crooks, moochers, vagrants, and famous people. I learned important things like the truth about hotel laundry—it costs more to launder something than it does to go out and buy another. I also learned that you should never make out with a drunk Italian guy in front of a boatload of Dutch tourists, because one of those tourists might turn out to be your grandmother. I learned that only supermodels look good in white bathing suits. I learned that most chicken sandwiches don't cost forty dollars. I learned that famous people are amazing parents, so amazing that they deserve many awards for their incredible parenting skills. I learned that sometimes it's better to be friends with normal, nonsupermodel people. I learned that ice cream in Italy is called gelato. I also learned that it's important never to throw a zaftig French art dealer's phone into the canal, even if you feel he double-crossed you with his wife (don't get me started).

I learned how to scam my parents for money in Venice. I learned how to put things on a house account in Venice (thus scamming my parents for money). I learned how to get a free ice cream in Venice (the whole Stew's photo incident). I learned how to say the Lord's Prayer in Italian in Venice (something my Jewish grandmother was really thrilled with). In Venice I learned that famous people are very interested in their children, so interested, in fact, that they hire numerous nannies to monitor their children and report back to them. I learned that writers are better parents than socialites. I learned that socialites are better parents than movie stars. I learned that famous people can say only the names of other famous people and not the names of unfamous people. I learned this life lesson from the famous socialite who called me only Molly Jong. I learned that food at craft service tables can be very good. Did I mention that really what I learned in Venice was that famous people are the best parents out there? I know it's true. I read it in *People* magazine.

grandpa

*

MOST NEW YORK MEDIA TYPES were sure that Howard Fast was dead, but he wasn't, he was just living in Greenwich, Connecticut, with his secretary, who had recently become his wife, and his eleven-year-old stepson. "You know, Johnny," Grandpa would say to my dad during those last six months, "Jews leave their money to their children, you know that, Johnny. Yes, Johnny, Jews leave their money to their children." Luckily, Dad was smart enough to decode what that meant. It meant, "I'm leaving everything to my new wife." Which six months later he did.

In the last six months of Grandpa's life, Dad would call me up every week and say, "Moll, this is it. You have to get down here and visit Grandpa, because Grandpa is failing." And he always was, more and more each time. Grandpa was failing and Dad was preparing for the end. Dad was trying to forgive Grandpa.

The first last visit I made to him was in April 2002. He sat on the beige leather sofa that he'd owned for forty years. I couldn't even imagine owning anything for forty years. Grandpa always smoked, though he went through various periods of hiding it and not. Sometimes he'd smoke a pipe, sometimes cigars; mostly, though, as he got older he smoked cigarillos, thin, brown cigars the size of a cigarette. Grandpa's new wife smoked fistfuls of cigarettes, and this inspired Grandpa to do the same, even though he was struggling with emphysema.

"You know, *The New York Times* hates me," he said, lighting a cigar and leaning back. His clothing was all incredibly old. His shirts had burns on them. I remembered some of those old, pilling cardigans from the times when I would stay at my grandparents' for the weekend and he would wake me at six every morning with the sound of typewriter keys banging away. He didn't work every morning anymore. He didn't wake up at six anymore. He didn't even really write books anymore. He couldn't because of the strokes in his brain and the Parkinson's.

I started to laugh a little. "I don't think they hate you, Grandpa. You've gotten good reviews from them. Remember the review you got for *The Dinner Party?*"

He ignored me, and I remember wondering if it was normal to be obsessing about *The New York Times Book Review* on your almost deathbed. Was it normal? What about *The Atlantic* or the *London Review of Books*; were they not worthy

outlets? "So tell me, how's your work?" Grandpa said, dragging in on a cigarillo.

"Well, I'm working on—"

"They don't review my books anymore, the damn *New
York Times.*"

"How are you feeling, Grandpa?"

"Do you know any publishers who'd be interested in my
book on pacifism?"

"Well, we could send it to Ryan" (my ex-boyfriend, who
was at the time a junior editor at Plume).

"Yes, Ryan. I always liked Ryan. Why don't you see
Ryan anymore? Ryan was a good man. A writer always needs
an editor."

I agreed, and stayed awhile longer to smoke a cigarette
and drink some diet Coke before I drove back into New York
City.

The next time I came he was exactly the same; maybe a
month had elapsed, and it was May. He wore an old cardigan
over an even older polo shirt. He was so skinny all the veins
in his neck popped out. A year earlier I had really annoyed
my dad by trying to get Grandpa to tell me his life story.
I hadn't read any of his books, or his memoir. But I had
thought that since the novel I had been working on since
2000 was clearly an unpublishable mess, I might as well write
about what I had going. I had an idea that I'd write a heart-
breaking work of staggering genius aptly titled "Fridays with
Howie." This short novel would sit on the bestseller list, thus
making me famous enough to win the love of the aforementioned Howie.

The major problems with "Fridays with Howie" boiled

down to two things: (1) Howie was no Morrie (he wasn't no Peace Corps volunteer), and (2) Grandpa Howie loved to lie. From his promise to take my little brothers on the *QE2* (he never traveled) to his pledge that an old stamp collection was worth enough to put both of my little brothers through college, Grandpa had a bit of a reality problem. I think much of my father's life he thought he was going crazy because Grandpa was constantly lying about the most mundane and unnecessary things, which is how we know he's a writer. Often Dad and I would have a chuckle when a foreign news crew would come over and interview Grandpa for some documentary, because we just knew that 65 percent of everything he said was either a major exaggeration or a total fabrication.

The second visit was much like the first. Grandpa asked, "Why does *The New York Times* hate me?"

They don't. Proof of this can be seen in this quote from his obituary in *The New York Times*: "But Mr. Fast's breakthrough came in 1943 with *Citizen Tom Paine,* which the playwright Elmer Rice called, in a highly favorable front-page review in *The New York Times Book Review,* 'a vivid portrait of one of the most extraordinary figures of the eighteenth century.' "

"They never cover my work," Grandpa said.

"But—"

"Matt Damon wants me to write a movie for him." Grandpa lit another cigarillo. He was smoking more and more.

"That's—"

"Do you know any editors who might be interested in a book on pacifism?"

I took a sip of my diet Coke. "Umm, well, maybe you could have . . ."

And so it went with Grandpa Howie. He was nicer to me than to almost anyone else. He was chock-full of ambivalence toward his children. He resented and tortured both his wives in weirdly passive-aggressive ways. He had very mixed feelings toward his new wife's children, whom he often called "animals." But with me he was always wonderful. This can be explained by these facts: I was pretty, I was related to Erica Jong, and I had published a novel when I was twenty-one. Of course he had published a novel at eighteen, so he wasn't that impressed with the precociousness of the act, though he did still respect me for my proximity to fame that was not his (Mom's fame). In some ways I loved Grandpa Howie more than anyone I'd ever known; in spite of his lying, his honesty was inescapable. That said, he was, like all famous people, completely obsessed with getting and staying famous. Think of the Peace Corps volunteers who are catapulted to fame or the gardeners who suddenly find themselves on the cover of *Vogue*.

Now I had gotten a bad review in *The New York Times,* but I had been thrilled because it was a large review taking up a whole page. Grandpa had been infuriated. He had been enraged. He had been inflamed. Mom had thought it was amusing and had the review framed for me. But Grandpa had written a letter to *The New York Times Book Review.* A letter which, thank God, was never published. The letter said something to the effect of "I, Howard Fast, am the author of seventy-five books. I have been writing for sixty-seven years. I am a bestselling author. My books have been published the world over. I think Molly Jong-Fast deserved a better review. She is my granddaughter, and while she is not by any means a great writer, she is a good writer. Some might say a very good writer. I would not say that, but she is a pretty good writer. And after all, she was only twenty-one when her book came out. Of course I was eighteen when my first book came out. . . ." (Remember, I am writing this from that shaky place called my rather drug-ravaged memory, but this is pretty accurate.)

Then something happened: Grandpa went into the hospital. He had another stroke. The congestive heart failure was getting really bad. This was in August.

"You know, I'm dying," he said as we sat together in Greenwich Hospital. I hated Greenwich Hospital. Just as I hated Greenwich, a town where streets are named after Lauders and where a black person driving a car is automatically stopped and strip-searched.

Grandpa had been in and out of the hospital for the last five years. He had emphysema, congestive heart failure, small strokes in the brain, Parkinson's, and the beginning of Alzheimer's. He was 88 years old. What did he think? Did he think he was supposed to live to be 110 despite his emphysema and his refusal to stop chain-smoking? When I looked at him, I hoped he would die. He had lived so long that he was depriving the rest of us. With many famous people there can be only one star, but with Grandpa there could be only one human, one person who got the air, food, and water. His second wife was tired. I was tired. Dad was tired. Auntie Rachel was tired. Even Grandpa was tired.

But the larger problem was that Grandpa was old, so old

that death really wasn't tragic, it was inevitable. Grandpa was a novelist, so he didn't want an undramatic death. Don't get me wrong, his first choice was to not die at all, but his second choice was a tragic death. Sadly, eighty-eight-year-olds don't have tragic deaths.

We weren't supposed to contradict him when he said he was dying, because the fact that he was starting to see this happening to him was actually a huge step in the right direction. "Yes, I think you are, Grandpa."

He leaned back in the little hospital bed. He was angry to be in the hospital and had already tried to pull all his tubes out. "Why does *The New York Times* hate me? Why?"

"I don't think they do."

He wouldn't argue with me. He'd just move on to something else. "How's Ryan?" Any normal Jewish grandparent would be happy I'd left the goy to be with nice, Jewish Matt Greenfield.

"He's good, I guess."

"You know, he would love my book on pacifism."

"Really?"

And so it went with Grandpa Howie.

A few weeks later, Grandpa collapsed at a labor rally and was brought into the hospital. I visited him again in Greenwich Hospital. Greenwich Hospital was the scene of my grandmother's final hospitalizations, seven years before. The outside of the hospital was made of rusting metal. In the lobby of the hospital, there was a piano that played music by itself. I parked in the underground garage. I saw Grandpa's new wife's car parked down there: the red sports car he never bought Grandma, the sports car Grandma never really wanted.

When I walked into the room, Grandpa was sitting in a chair. He wasn't wearing his glasses. He had oxygen tubes in his nose. He was hunched over. He was asleep. His round, bald head looked so soft. He looked so sweet. He looked like a baby. He didn't look like a Communist threat. He didn't look like someone with a ten-thousand-plus-page FBI file. He also didn't look like a threat to his children's sanity. The room smelled that normal hospital, antibacterial smell. Grandpa's new wife asked me to stay awhile with him, while she got some much-needed air. I said fine.

"Do you know anyone at *The New York Times Book Review*?" he asked me as soon as he woke up. I sat on the foot of the bed. His legs were in inflatable pants that kept inflating and deflating. The point of the inflatable pants was to keep him from getting blood clots in his legs. The sound of inflating and deflating pants was incredibly distracting.

"Just that guy, you know him too. But I don't think that—"

The pants inflated again. I wondered if he noticed. "What are you working on?"

"I'm working on a book of essays about my childhood." If we'd been a normal family, Grandpa could have said something to me about protecting the family secrets, but since Grandpa had written about cheating on Grandma in his memoirs and Mom had written about everything else in hers, there weren't any family secrets that hadn't been excerpted in *People* magazine.

He paused. "Have you seen Ryan lately?"

"No."

"How's your mother?"

"Good, she's got a new book coming out."

"Ohh really." He leaned back in his chair. Competition came into his eyes in a weird, slightly evil sparkle; it was one of the few things that reminded him he wasn't dead yet.

"Yes, it's on ancient Greece."

"Who's publishing it?"

"Norton."

"Did she get a big advance?"

"I don't know," I lied.

"How many cities is the tour?"

"Fifteen, I think."

"Oh." You could see in his eyes that he was doing the calculations. Grandpa knew what a fifteen-city tour meant, he knew the range of a Norton advance, he was factoring all those numbers and then weighing them against his own.

"I'm not sure, though."

"How's Ken?"

Writing is the one recourse of the disinherited child of the famous. But what my real intention is, what I'm really trying to explain, is why we loved Grandpa Howie even though he didn't want us to. Why Dad, Grandma, Belle (his second wife), Barbara (my stepmother), my uncle, my little brothers, and Auntie Rachel loved him so much more than he would have ever wanted.

I sat with him awhile longer. Every few minutes he'd completely lose his lucidity and scream, "Where is Belle? Where is Belle?"

"She's coming. I'm here now. She's coming." A granddaughter is no substitute.

"I need Belle," he'd cry.

I always hated those men who left their wives for younger models. In New York City it was the kind of thing I witnessed daily. But Grandpa didn't leave Grandma. In fact, Grandma left Grandpa. She died. In a family where fame was the goal of life, she never got famous. She never got recognized for her sculptures. She wasn't interested in getting famous, which is not to say that she didn't enjoy the by-products of Grandpa's fame. She liked staying at the Ritz in Paris just as much as the next person, but Grandma didn't have that crazy need, that psychotic fire that the rest of us had. Grandpa resented this on some level. There was a peace Grandma had that Grandpa didn't. In an effort to disturb that peace, Grandpa published posthumously a book of photographs of her sculptures with a vanity press. Grandma didn't get a big obituary. In fact, she got a small obituary and a small funeral, like a normal unfamous person.

Grandpa didn't die in the hospital that time. He held on. He came home. He started hallucinating and trying to kill Belle; his grip on her throat was sometimes surprisingly hard to dislodge. Which I guess means she deserves the inheritance. Is it wrong that I'm so bitter about what he did to my father and my aunt?

The last time I went to visit him was at the house. He was smoking. His skin looked very blue. He was out of it. He sat in the living room on the old brown sofa. He was trying to drink from a cup, and he kept spilling its contents on his lap.

Matt came, too. Matt had never met Grandpa. Dad and I took advantage of that and left Matt alone with Grandpa.

This was a cruel trick we often played on unsuspecting people. See, we knew that he was going to rattle on and on and on about himself, but newcomers might be intrigued by his ranting. They could listen to "Why does *The New York Times* hate me?" with a fresh ear.

Dad and I came back into the room after twenty minutes. Matt looked like he'd definitely had enough.

"Congratulations on your engagement. I'm sure you'll be very happy," Grandpa said, with a very slight tinge of bitterness.

"Thanks, Grandpa," I said as I leaned over and kissed him.

Then, in the vein of a Godfather movie, Grandpa leaned toward us and said, "You have my blessing."

He died a week later. We were all very relieved. *The New York Times* ran an enormous obituary that took up almost the whole page. The headline was "Howard Fast, Best-Selling Novelist, Dies at 88." The first paragraph read:

Howard Fast, whose best-selling historical fiction often featured the themes of freedom and human rights, elements in his own tumultuous political journey through the blacklisting of the 1950's, died yesterday at his home in Old Greenwich, Conn. He was 88.

I guess it turned out that *The New York Times* didn't hate him after all. But why did Grandpa think that *The New York Times* hated him? It turns out that someone crazier than Grandpa told Grandpa that sometime in the 1950s there was a *New York Times* editorial board meeting where some editors (who were then rumored to be Trotskyites) said they wouldn't run articles on Grandpa because he was a Marxist. This story, like many of the stories Grandpa based much of his life on, is totally unsubstantiated.

But enough about Trotsky, let's get back to the memoirist's job of settling the score. Of course I (and the other grandchildren) weren't mentioned in my grandpa's obit. The only people mentioned were his children (Dad and Auntie Rachel) and his stepchildren; after all, he had known them for four years (I think I need to go back into therapy). Afterward I would tastefully joke that I wasn't famous enough to get into Grandpa's obit. People were somewhat distressed by this joke, which is why I love it.

Grandpa's funeral was held in the temple in Greenwich, Connecticut, where we had held Grandma's funeral. The illustrious Rabbi Silverman presided. I had spent some time with Rabbi Silverman after the death of my grandmother. In November 1994, Grandpa and I had sat in Rabbi Silverman's office before Grandma's service.

"You know, I myself am no stranger to fame," Rabbi Silverman had said, sitting at his desk in his huge office in his hugely wealthy synagogue in Greenwich, Connecticut. "Yes, I know quite a lot about the pressures of fame. My son is a famous movie star." Rabbi Silverman leaned back in his large leather chair and pointed to the pictures of his son. "Fame is a funny, funny thing, a fickle mistress even."

Now let me just state in the vague interest of accuracy that the rabbi's son wasn't exactly a movie star, though he was the star of both *Weekend at Bernie's* and *Weekend at Bernie's II.*

But Rabbi Silverman had inadvertently brought up an interesting point, which was that being a writer is a lot like being in a movie where you play second to a corpse.

He pointed to pictures of his son standing with other famous people. He was a big, Jewish rabbi–looking guy. "But about Bette's funeral," Grandpa said.

"He's starring in a big movie coming on this spring."

It was about seven years later, and here I was again in the presence of the illustrious Rabbi Silverman. Also presiding at Grandpa's funeral was Belle's local Catholic priest. A priest was particularly apropos, since we're all Jewish and Grandpa loathed the Catholic Church more than he loathed all the other faiths combined. But history is written by the young second wives who survive, not by the people who suffer their whole lives with the deceased. In the end the local Catholic priest really wasn't so bad.

But what was bad, what was really, really, really bad, was that Belle had mass cards made up with pictures of Grandpa on them and prayers to Jesus on the back. She handed them out in the temple. They were like little Grandpa Howie and Jesus baseball cards. Perhaps there was a collectible aspect that I was missing. They had a prayer to Jesus on them. Now, we Jews just aren't that into Jesus. We don't believe in Jesus. Grandma Bette, the soul of good taste, could have lived through the Catholic priest, she could have lived through Rabbi Silverman's "Death is a destination and life is a journey" speech, but Grandma Bette never in a million years would have been able to survive mass cards.

Belle spoke very well. My stepmom spoke, and she was fantastic too. My little brothers were adorable and sweet (both brothers are still single and half Jewish). My little brothers and I and Belle's kids were the pallbearers. I was really shocked by how heavy the casket was.

Then we put him in the ground and it was all over. It was so odd to leave him there in Norwalk next to Grandma. Belle did a wonderful thing: when the funeral home volunteered to dig Grandma up and move her over so that Belle could someday spend eternity next to Grandpa in the Jewish cemetery in Norwalk, Connecticut, Belle said no to digging up her predecessor. While this merely sounds like common decency, in this context it is actually a genuine mitzvah. And so they didn't dig up Grandma. They just let her be, which after a lifetime with Grandpa, was really the least they could do.

Grandpa wasn't an alcoholic. He wasn't addicted to speed or heroin. He didn't beat or sexually abuse his children, but it's not exactly clear that he ever loved them either. He never killed anyone; he was a pacifist. He was a Buddhist. He meditated almost every day. He practiced Zen. He went before the House Un-American Activities Committee and refused to name names, thus sentencing himself to both jail time and the blacklist. Grandpa was a left-wing hero. Grandpa was obsessed with the condition of the poor, the working classes. Grandpa had many admirable beliefs. But none of that helped him to be nicer to his family.

In the end this huge force who had wreaked havoc on all the lives around him was left in the Jewish cemetery in Norwalk to decompose. None of his books, none of his movies, none of the articles about him, none of those documentary filmmakers were buried with him; Grandpa went alone into that dark night.

Grandpa died. Which was something he really didn't want to happen to him. But at least he got a big, flattering obituary, thus proving (just a few days too late) that *The New York Times* didn't hate him. All in all, I think Grandpa Howie is an excellent role model for me as both a writer and a human being. I hope that someday *The New York Times* will write a flattering obituary about me.